The House
on an
Irish
Hillside

Felicity Hayes-McCoy was born in Dublin, Ireland. She read English and Irish language and literature at UCD before moving to England in the 1970s to train at The Drama Studio, London. Her work as a writer includes television and radio drama, features, documentaries, dramatisations and adaptations; screenplays; music theatre; children's books, and interactive multimedia product.

She and her husband, opera director Wilfred Judd, live in Corca Dhuibhne and in Bermondsey, London. She blogs about life in both places on her website:

www.felicityhayesmccoy.co.uk

The House on an Irish Hillside

Felicity Hayes-McCoy

HODDER &
STOUGHTON

First published in Great Britain in 2012 by Hodder & Stoughton
An Hachette UK company

1

A CIP catalogue record for this title is
available from the British Library

ISBN 978 1 444 73030 2
eBook ISBN 978 1 444 73033 3

Typeset by Palimpsest Book Production Ltd, Falkirk, Stirlingshire

Printed and bound in Great Britain by Clays Ltd, St Ives plc

Hodder & Stoughton policy is to use papers that are natural,
renewable and recyclable products and made from wood grown in
sustainable forests. The logging and manufacturing processes are expected
to conform to the environmental regulations of the country of origin.

Hodder & Stoughton Ltd
338 Euston Road
London NW1 3BH

www.hodder.co.uk

Le buíochas agus mór-mheas,
do
Sheán Ó Flatharta
agus do
mhuintir Chorca Dhuibhne uilig

To
Jack Flaherty
and
the people of Corca Dhuibhne,
with thanks and respect

Contents

Introduction

This book tells my story. I'm writing it in Ireland, in a house on a hillside. The house sits low in the landscape between a holy well and the site of an Iron Age dwelling. It was built of stones ploughed out of the fields by men who knew how to raise them with their hands and to lock one stone to the next so each was firm. It's a lone house on the foothills of the last mountain on the Dingle peninsula, the westernmost point in mainland Europe. At night the sky curves above it like a dark bowl, studded with stars.

The peninsula has a high mountain spine running

westwards into the Atlantic Ocean and rising again as seven islands, called the Blaskets. The Atlantic waves are white where they curl against the cliffs. Farther out they're turquoise, shimmering emerald and pale jade, their colours constantly changed by the shadows of drifting clouds. The end of the peninsula is nine miles long, six miles across at its widest and three where it's narrowest. These last few miles, beyond the fishing port of Dingle, are known to the locals as 'back west'.

It's a place of music and memories. Every gathering leads to music, songs and stories, handed down through generations in the musical Irish language. Today, everyone in Ireland speaks English. Often tourists come and go without taking in the fact that an Irish language exists. But it does. Here in Ireland it's called Irish, never Gaelic. And here on the extreme end of the peninsula it's the language of everyday life.

I grew up in Dublin, spoke English and loved books. I went on to study literature and now I write plays and books myself. But my first memories of stories and drama are rooted in a world in which people shared their experiences without writing things down. The roots of that world are in this place, where ideas, skills, beliefs and traditions have been passed on across thousands of years by word of mouth.

I first came to Dingle aged seventeen, on a scholarship to learn Irish. From the moment I crossed the mountain,

I fell in love with the place, which was more beautiful than any I'd ever seen. And with a way of looking at life that was deeper, richer and wiser than any I'd known before. It was something I'd glimpsed in my childhood in Dublin, a city kid curled on my country granny's bed listening to stories. I'd begun to understand it as a student, ploughing through books and exams. And then, on that first visit, I encountered it as reality. Rooted in rhythms and memories, powerful, dynamic and exciting, I found a shared vision of a world of balance and contentment.

Thirty years later I found this house here and my own share in that vision. In the years between I'd moved to London, become an actress and married my husband, Wilf. For more than half my lifetime, work and life led me away from this place where narrow roads wind between flowering ditches and the shadows of high clouds drift on the mountains. But from the first day I came here I always knew I'd come back.

As I write this now, listening to birds singing in the garden, the thirty years it took to find this house seem like nothing. Less than nothing. Time works differently here. In my neighbours' memory the difference between tens, hundreds and thousands of years hardly seems to matter; life moves to the circular rhythm of the seasons, and past, present and future are just spokes in a turning wheel. The landscape here is ancient. Patterns of ancient fields still mark the mountains. The memory of ancient buildings is printed on the earth, where grass and growth are subtly different over hidden foundation stones. The stories and songs I hear now by my fireside are echoes of ancient voices.

In Irish the peninsula's name is *Corca Dhuibhne*. It's pronounced something like Curk-uh-gwee-nuh, and it means 'the territory of the people of the goddess Danú'. Danú's people were Celts who came to Ireland from mainland Europe and Britain, probably moving ahead of the advancing Roman Empire. They farmed the fields outside my windows and hunted in forests that have long since crumbled to turf. They were subtle, creative people who rated poets and craftsmen with kings. They saw death as pregnant with life. They loved colour and detail, repeated patterns and images, dynamic contrasts, grotesque humour and turning points in stories and in life. They revelled in words shaped and strung together to make music out of imagery. Their customs and traditions, the gods they imagined and the values they held still shape my neighbours' lives. Here ancient stories are remembered, told and retold; they're starting points for argument and analysis, discussion and debate. And they all spiral round two central ideas: that all things are contained within all other things, and that everything in the universe shares a living soul.

For more than half my life Corca Dhuibhne was a place I escaped to, first on my own and then with Wilf. I used to dream of it when I was in London, squashed into a tube train or struggling through crowds to get to meetings. Soon after I moved to London I started writing as well as acting, and as I dashed from theatres to sound studios and rushed home to my desk to face the next deadline, I'd imagine days spent on roads between flowering ditches, the shadows of the clouds drifting out over the ocean, and evenings lying on clifftops, watching the sun set over the Atlantic. Wilf and I came here on our honeymoon. From then on it became our refuge when life got tough.

Whenever we could we'd make a dash for Dingle. There was the battle with London traffic to get to the airport, the brief flight, the blissful smell of the air as the cabin door opened, and the short walk from the plane to the arrivals hall. Then we'd hire a car, drive over the mountain and sink into familiar chairs by familiar fires. Later, we'd wander out of our B&B and eat clam chowder and bacon and cabbage in a restaurant by the pier. Then we'd walk the streets, or drive back west, till we heard music, and join a couple of fiddlers and a piper round a table in a pub.

Then one night we were staying back west, in Gorman's guesthouse, and something happened. Looking back, it feels like one minute we were relaxing by the fire and the next minute a vision of a different future had suddenly sparked between us. Every time we'd come back to Corca

Dhuibhne we'd felt at home. Did that mean that in fact we should be living here?

Síle, our hostess, was doubtful at first. 'I've seen it before,' she said, 'people come here on holiday, the weather's good and they're feeling relaxed. So suddenly they think they can escape from who they are and live the good life here instead.'

I wondered if she was right. Were we those people? What difference would it make to our lives if we did have a home here? It's not as if people in Corca Dhuibhne don't worry, have family feuds and political arguments and struggle with bills and mortgages, just like everyone else. But, as Wilf and I talked about it, we realised we weren't looking for escape any more. We weren't making a choice between two places or two ways of life. We wanted to live and work in both, to explore the dynamic contrasts between them and the light each sheds on the other. We made that choice, and it's changed our lives utterly.

The internet's the thing that makes it possible. It's the virtual space that links the two places and allows us both to work in either. Nowadays practically everyone in Corca Dhuibhne's got broadband and mobile phones. Kids text each other in English and Irish. My neighbours are web designers, hotel owners, builders, teachers. Some are musicians with international recording careers. But the same people are also beekeepers, farmers and fishermen.

It's still a place where people know how to plough fields, sow seed and reap harvests, to build stone walls and respect tradition. Here everyone's song or story is equally important. It's a place where people value community and celebrate individuality. And a place where music and storytelling have a central place in a communal, shared inheritance. For us that was crucial. Music is Wilf's thing. Story's mine.

The Irish have always been voyagers, which is why an estimated seventy million people across the world have Irish roots. For centuries ships have sailed from Irish ports carrying emigrants; adventurers, scholars and soldiers, monks, rebels and poets, people running from hunger and families chasing their dreams. Each of those journeys began with a decision and a first step on a road. That night in Síle Gorman's I realised I'd reached a turn in a long road I'd been walking for over half a lifetime. It had taken me here to Corca Dhuibhne in the first place, and then led me to London, where I'd found Wilf. Now it seemed to be leading me full circle. But this time it would take me far deeper into this place that held my heart. Sitting by Síle's turf fire, I remembered a saying I'd heard as a child. 'When you understand where you've come from you'll be able to see where you're going.' I didn't understand yet, and I didn't know how much finding this house on a hillside would change my way of seeing things. But I was going to find out.

1

The House on the Hillside

The day after that conversation, we started looking. The plan was to buy the site first and build the house later, when we had the money. But then, as we looked, we became more and more convinced that building wasn't the way to go. We didn't want a holiday home. We needed a place we could come to all year round. Besides, the peninsula already had too many new houses. In winter their large, plate glass windows stare blankly out at the raging Atlantic, while older houses, built by locals, nestle in more sheltered places protected from wind and storms. So we started looking for an old house we might buy and then work on ourselves.

It was going to mean seriously stringent budgeting. Each time we came back to Corca Dhuibhne we'd drive round searching, but whatever we found was always too dear or too derelict. Then, one day on our way to the airport for a flight back to London, we stopped in town for lunch and found three more possibilities. The least likely one was a low house, painted pale yellow. From its photo it seemed to have no garden, and it looked as if it might be built right on a road. But it sort of ticked some of our boxes – away from the sea views and main roads that might get built up over time, just about affordable, and within twenty minutes' walk of a pint of milk. We collected its details and shoved them into our luggage along with the other two, more likely, 'possibles'. Then we had our last plates of Dingle Bay prawns and brown soda bread, and drove across the mountain to the airport.

After a few weeks in London, Wilf found some free days and flew back to check out the 'possibles'. He rang me after the first day's viewings, sounding depressed. 'One's lovely but it's just too much work for me.' We'd already decided that our budget meant DIY. 'What about the other one?' 'Plot's too small to put in a septic tank.' Because of modern building regulations, drains were a problem in lots of the old houses we'd seen, particularly when the fields that used to belong to them had been sold off separately. I could tell from Wilf's voice he'd decided to call it a day. 'Has it started to rain?' 'Buckets,' he said, and rang off.

Sitting in London, I imagined him driving back west to Síle's through the rain and drying off in front of the fire before dinner. Whenever we ate at Gorman's we had fish, happy to order whatever Vincent, Síle's husband, suggested. When your chef was raised a fisherman he knows the best of the catch. As I put down the phone I could practically smell the turf fire and Vincent's perfectly cooked, freshly caught monkfish, salmon or scallops, served with vegetables from the garden and Síle's home-made bread. Peeved, and feeling a bit depressed myself, I went back to my computer.

Then, later that night when I was halfway through a bowl of pasta, Wilf rang me again. 'You know that yellow house?' 'Yes.' 'Well, you know what's just happened?' This time I could tell by his voice that it was good. He'd driven back to Gorman's, changed his wet clothes and sat by the fire. The photo of the yellow house had got tucked into the newspaper he'd brought with him to read. As he sat there, Maria, who helped at Gorman's, arrived to say dinner was ready. Wilf stood up and the photo slipped from between the pages of the newspaper. Sure that the yellow house would be no better than the rest, he'd turned to throw the photo on the fire. Then Maria leaned over and took it out of his hand.

Half an hour later, on a crackly phone line, I could hear his excitement. 'Maria says it's just up from her own house. It's in farmland. And it's set right back from the road, in a garden. It's surrounded by hedges.' That didn't sound right to me. 'How come there's not even a blade of grass in the photo, then?' 'I don't know, I suppose they were featuring the house. Anyway, Maria says it's a beautiful road and the house is set back on a corner. And there are ash trees.' Now it sounded as if he ought to see it, so I asked if he was going to make an appointment. 'I've done it.' 'What, at nine o'clock at night?' 'I've talked to the man who owns it.' It had all been incredibly easy. 'I phoned, he picked up and it's all fixed. I'm meeting him tomorrow.'

Next day he rang me from his mobile. I could hear birdsong in the background. 'I'm here.' 'Where?' 'In the garden.' 'There is a garden, then?' 'Oh, there's definitely a garden.' He was standing in front of the house, surrounded by wildflowers and waving grasses and shaggy hedges of fuchsia and arbutus. As he walked the boundary, describing the ash trees, the angle of the low house to the road and the steep fields rearing behind it, I could hear sheep calling on the mountain.

We were used to the cut-throat London property market where nothing's secured without money, and prices suddenly shoot up at the last minute, forcing buyers to rework their finances or lose their purchase. But when

Lasse, the owner, had heard our story and we'd shown him round, he'd simply shaken Wilf's hand and said he wouldn't consider any other offers till I'd seen the house. Then, as he left with his six-month-old baby asleep on his shoulder, he handed Wilf the key, suggesting he might like to take some photos for me to look at in London. 'And keep the key till she comes over. Then you can make your minds up in peace.'

After Wilf and I talked on the phone he went back into the house with his camera, trying to capture the feel as well as the layout. After that he drove up the hill and down, taking views from the fields and the roads. Then he went back to the garden and struggled through high grass, hedges and bushes, taking shots of the house from all angles. At the top of the garden, choked by briars and bindweed, he found three little wind stunted apple trees. And in the grass under a fuchsia bush he found fragments of a half buried, broken pot, glazed in smoky bands of purple-grey and speckled aquamarine.

He brought a shard of that pot back to London, along with the photos. I'd like to say that when I saw them I was flooded with joy. Actually, I was flooded with a deep sense of exhaustion and burst into tears. I could see that the house was perfect for us. The single living room had been partitioned to make a hallway, but restored to its original size it would be a high room with a boarded ceiling and perfect acoustics for music. The interior walls had been panelled, but underneath they were still rough plaster, and the chimney on the north gable wall hadn't been blocked up. The two tiny bedrooms against the other gable could be made into one larger room and a separate deskspace. A tiny 1970s extension at the rear could become a tiny fitted kitchen. The loo and the shower needed work, but that could be done. The roof was leaking, but that could be fixed. Riotous pink hydrangeas were trying to force their way through every window, but they could be subdued. The hedges blocked views of the mountains, but they could be trimmed. The septic tank was an issue, but that could be resolved. For our purposes, the whole house needed rewiring and replumbing, but we'd been there before. And Wilf was upbeat and excited, longing to begin.

Typically, I started to obsess over all the reasons why we shouldn't buy it. Equally typically, he'd already started working out ways and means. But once we'd decided to look for an old house, our plan depended on my continuing to write in London and Wilf taking a career break here, to work on it. So all I could see were the months of separation ahead of us, when he'd be teetering on ladders in Corca Dhuibhne and I'd be working in London, waiting to hear he'd fallen off.

But even as I sat dripping tears on his photos I knew I was being a wimp. This was our chance and we weren't going to get a better one. So we cleared the next few days and flew over for me to see the house. I remember Wilf's face as we drove up the hill. He was determined not to put pressure on me. We slowed down as we passed a farm where hens were pecking at watercress by a stream. There were dogs outside, and a cat stalked down from the cowshed as we passed. We drove on up the hill. If you take that road now, you can see our house from the turn above the farm. But then it was hidden by hedges, and we nearly missed the entrance. When we'd reversed and parked we opened the five barred gate and went into the garden. Birds rustled in the hedges. We could hear bees droning in the clover blossoms and a blackbird cried out in alarm. There was a flash of black wings and yellow beak, and he was gone.

I looked at the house. It was built a hundred years ago, a plain, grey, single storied building with a central front door. A rickety porch with a sloping corrugated roof had been built on, to protect the door from the wind. The coat of yellow paint had happened later. There was a chimney at each gable end, adding to the tranquil symmetry of the door and its balancing windows, even though the windows themselves had been slightly enlarged and the original sash frames were gone. I could see that a couple of slates had shifted on the roof, but the ridge was still straight and sound. The hysterically pink hydrangeas growing against the walls were anything but tranquil. Here and there, a blazing blue one added a shrill, incidental note to the effect of a noisy crowd jostling to get in. But the house itself – built low to the ground and flanked by a little shed against its north gable – had an air of strength and calm. Still carefully avoiding putting pressure on me, Wilf opened the front door and we went in. He needn't have worried. I already knew we were home.

We never gave the key back to Lasse. Instead we bought the house on a second handshake and Wilf moved in to start the work, with two camp chairs, a mattress and a new transistor radio. And I continued to dodge over and back whenever I could, turning up at meetings in London with increasingly battered hands and broken nails.

It wasn't easy. We'd been used to spending our working days together, so being alone in the London house felt strange. If you work from home you have to create patterns for your own days, otherwise you never get anything done. When Wilf and I had been together in London we'd shared tea breaks and arranged our days' work round practical domestic things, like who'd go out to the supermarket or stay home to take deliveries. We'd plan walks, go to concerts and the theatre, and make sure we had two days off a week, even if they weren't always at weekends. But living on my own I was in danger of sitting at my desk all day without eating and then suddenly discovering there was no food in the house. I remember turning off the TV and going out for walks at midnight, having realised I hadn't been out of doors for twenty-four hours.

One day when I nipped out for milk I encountered a couple of neighbours. Ellie, a doe-eyed advertising executive with implants and a lot of shiny bronzer, asked me how I was. 'Fine,' I said, intent on getting my milk before the tea I'd just made went cold. 'And do you see Wilf much?' she asked, registering concern. 'Er, yeah, I saw him last week. And we talk on the phone.' She nodded kindly. Paula, who was brisker, asked if I was getting out at all. 'Well, I'm working, you know, and it's kind of difficult . . .' Ellie put her hand on my arm, 'you need to start networking,' she said gently. I must have looked blank. 'Really,' she said. 'You've got to find your own life. But it's great that you and Wilf can still be friends.' Still focused on what I'd been writing, I smiled and backed away. Ten minutes later, drinking tea at the kitchen table, I burst out laughing. I'd just realised that, as far as the gossips were concerned, Wilf was basking in the Bahamas with a chorus girl.

Instead of which he was plumbing and wiring, sawing and sanding, filing and filling, effing and blinding, and knocking up endless buckets of sand and cement. And in the evenings, after a meal eaten from the top of his Black and Decker Workmate, he'd slump in front of the fire with the radio, before crashing out on a mattress on the floor. Each time I visited, my heart bled for him. I hated going back and leaving him there alone. But working on his own, asking advice about where to get tools and materials, sitting on his camp chair in front of the open fire or going down to the pub in the evenings, he met our new neighbours. The pace was right, and, looking back, I know it was the best way we could have gone about it. In Corca Dhuibhne time works differently. And neighbours matter.

Jack Flaherty lives in the farm down the hill. Wilf and I met him together, on the first day we'd arrived here, when he walked up the road with his dogs. He enquired our names, told us his own and we stood in the garden and talked. The next day, as we walked past his gate he invited us in. He had two dogs then, Spot and Sailor, and a cat who could open doors and ate cabbage. Sailor was getting old. He liked to lean against Jack's knees by the range, with his muzzle in Jack's hand. Wilf and I sat at the kitchen table. The cat lay on Spot's back and Spot lay on the floor. We talked for a few minutes about the weather and the people who lived in the village. Then Jack made a pot of tea. I leant back with a mug in my hands, looking out through the open door at three red hens pecking cress by the stream. Outside I could hear voices calling on the mountain. And as we sat there Jack told us a story.

The house is ours, bought and paid for, but in this place where other values take precedence, it's still called *Tí Neillí Mhuiris*. Jack told us why. Tí Neillí Mhuiris means Neillí Muiris's house. Neillí and her mother had it from the time it was built a hundred years ago from stones ploughed out of the fields. It had three rooms then, and a wide hearth in the north gable where Neillí cooked her meals on the open fire. Muiris was Neillí's father. Paddy was her husband but he 'married in', so the house was always called hers. They grew their food on the mountain behind it, kept animals in the stone sheds outside, and cut turf to fuel the fire on a high strip of bog that's still known as theirs. They had no children but the neighbours' kids ran in to visit and Neillí gave them biscuits from a tin she kept under the bed. My bed stands in the same place today and I turn the same earth in the garden outside.

Paddy was a fisherman. He had a dog that used to sit up at the table when he and Neillí were eating. He was always afraid the wind would lift the roof. So he put a whiskey bottle two thirds full of water upside down into a two-pound marmalade jar and used the changing water levels in the bottle to predict the weather. People here still argue about whether it worked.

It was Paddy who planted the three ash trees that shelter our gable from the Atlantic storms. But it takes more than one man's lifetime for an ash to grow tall enough to turn the wind. So when winter gales rolled in off the ocean Paddy would leave the fireside to Neillí and sit in the byre with the beasts. I suppose that having fished the Atlantic in tarred canvas boats he had a healthy respect for the power of the wind. The byre, built against a high earth bank, must have sheltered him like a cave. When he got older he'd sometimes complain that his heart was bad and want to be taken to hospital. Everyone knew he just panicked when the sky threatened storms. But the fear was real and he was old, so the hospital always took him in for the night and sent him home to Neillí in the morning.

Since that day in Jack's kitchen I've learnt more about this house. I know, because neighbours have told us, that Paddy and Neillí's chimney smoked so badly that kids running in for a biscuit couldn't see the fireplace from the door. I know that when Neillí died she left pages covered with songs she'd written. They were songs about the rent man and the cost of food, and life in her stone house where her door was always open and our neighbours now still come to talk and sing.

When Neillí and Paddy died the house went to Lís and her husband Con, who was a great gardener, then to Biddy, who was a nurse, and then to Lasse, his wife Emer and Líobhán. I know those names now, and the stories that link them to the house. And I've learnt that it's my duty to remember them. Memory matters here. So does who you are and where you came from.

Líobhán was the baby asleep on Lasse's shoulder when Lasse and Wilf shook hands in the garden and Wilf took the key to the house. By Lasse's time the fireplace was no longer used for cooking and the smoky chimney had been fixed by a new flue. There's electricity and gas now, and water's pumped to the bathroom shower and the kitchen sink. But Neillí would know the taste of it. It still comes straight from the mountain.

In a field across our road the same water rises in a holy well. For thousands of years it's bubbled into a stone hollow, where people came to pray for healing. People still come there. If you turn right outside our gate and walk down past Jack's farm you'll join a pilgrim's way called the Saints' Road. People walk it still. The Saints' Road is Christian and medieval and the holy well is pagan and prehistoric. This has always been a place for learning and healing, where ritual is remembered and passed on.

And it's a place where community and individuality are equally important. Between our garden and the road a stream runs in a deep ditch, shaded by ferns. In a field on the other side of the road is a derelict house. There was a woman who lived there who was also called Neillí.

When I first asked about the two Neillís people said little. 'They were both strong women,' they'd say. Or 'there were times you'd hear them exchanging their opinions.' Later I heard other stories. There was the day the two Neillís had a stand-off on the road. They'd met where only one could pass and neither would give way. I don't know who won in that stand-off, though I'd say the rest of the neighbours were laying bets. But a woman from up the hill told me how the two Neillís came together to dig holes in the banks of the stream between their houses, to store their butter and milk. The butter made here was salty and yellow. They'd wrap it in cloth and reach down through the curling ferns to cool places between the smooth stones. Human relationships are complex, and life in a close-knit community's full of subtleties and layers. But some things are simple. The same ferns still grow on those banks today. The same water flows outside my door.

The house across the road stands higher than ours and from its door you can look out towards the shifting Atlantic waves, turquoise blue or steel grey, depending on the colour of the sky. People say it was always a good dry house, but last winter the wind got under the roof slates. If nothing's done to save it, there'll soon be nothing left but four stone walls. Higher up on the mountain, in one of Jack's fields, are other tumbled stone walls, surrounding a circular shelter. Like the two Neillís' houses it was built of stones ploughed from the fields. But the stones in Jack's field were raised thousands of years ago. Some Iron Age family lived up there on the mountain, looking down at the sites of the two Neillís' houses, the holy well and the shifting Atlantic waves. And beneath that ancient family's tumbled walls is a stone lined hollow where they stored their butter and milk.

No one remembers the names of the people who built their house in Jack's field. But the same tradition that remembers Paddy and the two Neillís respects and acknowledges these other dead neighbours, who shared the same landscape and lived with the intense awareness of community that's alive here today.

For thousands of years, in a custom called *bothántaíocht,* people here have come together to talk, sing and play music. In Neillí's time Tí Neillí Mhuiris was a great house for a gathering. Paddy and Neillí sat by this hearth and sang songs that are still sung here now. These days people here will text each other to arrange music sessions and turn up with a bottle, and maybe an apple tart. In the same way, their grandparents used to turn up for nights of bothántaíocht with a sod of turf for the fire.

I poke the fire now, and when it draws well people laugh and recall Neillí flapping her apron as smoke poured into the room. Then I pour the tea, there's a knock on the door, and everyone makes room for the newcomers. John Kennedy from Dún Chaoin has brought us some honey. Talk turns to the beehives in the steep, sheltered garden behind his house. Then Jack remembers the wild bees' nests he used to find in the fields as a child. 'You'd dig them out with a stick to get the honey.' He'd found one in the field where his cows now graze round those tumbled Iron Age walls. Wilf and I found one last year in our garden. The dark brown honey tasted sweet and earthy. John Kennedy's honey tastes of the heather and furze on the mountain, where his bees 'drink the taste of the flowers'. The door opens again, and people make room for the musicians. Someone starts a tune, Wilf reaches under his chair for his concertina, and the fire's made up. Then the music takes over as the tea goes round again.

2

Crossing the Mountain

If you're driving to Dingle you cross mountains. Above you, and below, are moving clouds. You can stand on a high place under a clear sky with the sun on your face and clouds swirling at your feet. You can look down and see rainbows. And all around you is the living strength of earth, sea and sky.

Far below, beyond wisps of drifting cloud, is the tapering end of the peninsula, the cluster of offshore islands and the vast expanse of the Atlantic reaching to the horizon. The sky is curved like a bowl of air. You can taste the sea on the wind, and the honey smell of the heather and the coconut smell of yellow furze warmed by the sun. There's an ancient Irish belief in 'places of resurrection', where a spirit is happiest on earth and most in touch with eternity. The first time I crossed the mountains of Corca Dhuibhne I found my place of resurrection.

I was seventeen, here on a scholarship to study the Irish language. I'd set off from my home in Dublin in the morning by train. It was dusk when I crossed the mountain and dark by the time a rattling van drove me out back west. I thought I knew where I was going.

I knew I was looking for Hurley's farm near a place called An Charraigh. Being a student of Irish, I knew that *an charraigh* meant 'the rock'. But as I peered out into the darkness beyond the window, that didn't seem particularly helpful. The van dropped me at the roadside and rattled into the night. I was tired and anxious and I'd no idea where to go next. I had directions to the farmhouse on a piece of paper but it was too dark to read them. There were no lights anywhere.

As I stood there I realised that, as a city dweller, this was the first time I'd ever been alone with the night. It was terrifying. There seemed to be no edge to anything. There was just the darkness and myself. Somewhere high in the air, a faint difference between black and marginally less black suggested the huge presence of a mountain. Somehow that was terrifying too. I stood with one foot on tarmacadam while the other groped for a foothold in thick, rutted mud. Suddenly there was a gust of wind and I sensed, and then saw, pale puffballs of giant hogweed swaying on a ditch beside the road. The wind had shifted the clouds. Slowly my eyes began to adjust to glimmering starlight. I started to walk down the road. Then someone called my name, a torch flashed and a figure loomed out of the darkness. I couldn't see his face because of the torchlight. But his hand was warm and strong, and he told me I was welcome.

Hurley's farm was a grey two-storey house with barns and sheds behind it, built on the foothills of the mountain. As I followed Mr Hurley into the yard I could see lights in the windows and, as we approached, the door was opened from inside. The first thing I remember about Mrs Hurley was her gentle voice. She took my hands and welcomed me into her home. Mr Hurley carried my bag through to a bedroom at the back of the house. By the time I'd been given a cup of tea and a seat by the range he'd gone outside again to check on a heifer in calf.

As I leant back in my chair and stretched my legs to the fire I realised that one of my shoes was caked with mud from the roadside. Mrs Hurley's kitchen floor was spotless but she laughed away my apologies and propped the shoe against the edge of the range to dry. Mud wasn't important. Talk, warmth and comfort were.

When I look back on the rest of that evening I remember

a jumble of impressions and sensations. The hard wood under the soft cushion on my chair. The flames leaping up when Mrs Hurley poked the fire. The strong tea tasting strangely of creamy milk. An elderly lady wrapped in a dark shawl sitting by the range, in the seat tradition-ally kept for the oldest member of the household. I remember the light shining on a pot or a kettle beside her. She had deep-set eyes and the strong, handsome bone structure of many of the women on the peninsula. I remember Mrs Hurley's dark hair and her quiet voice speaking a richer, more musical Irish than I'd ever heard before. And the smell of turf smoke, heavy and fragrant, mixed with the warm smell of baking bread. For the first time since I'd set out that morning I felt completely relaxed.

My bed was warm and narrow, in a low, whitewashed room behind the kitchen. When I'd arrived the wind was rising but I slept at once. Sometime in the night I woke, aware of moonlight and a silence outside that seemed deeper than just the absence of sound. I had no dreams.

In the morning there was a tap on the door and Mrs Hurley's voice outside it. '*A Fhelicití, a chroí, tá roinnt bricfeasta ullamh anois agam duit, a chailín.*' 'Felicity, dear, I have a share of breakfast ready now for you, girl.' I woke to that same gentle, rhythmic call each day I spent in that house. It contains all the warmth and hospitality of Corca Dhuibhne. And embedded in that phrase 'roinnt bricfeasta' is the value system that informs how life here is lived. The food spread on the table wasn't my breakfast. It was my share of breakfast. When I got out of bed, aware that I was there to learn, I made a note of the Irish language idiom. It was years before I realised the phrase contained a deeper lesson.

Breakfast was a new laid egg, more strong tea and a pile of buttered toast. The window was propped open and outside I could hear a dog urging a herd of cows up to the field. When I'd eaten I stepped into the yard. It was a rain-washed morning with a sky like mother of pearl. I stood there with my back against the wall and my head tipped back in amazement. High up against the pale sky was the huge presence that I'd sensed the night before. Steep foothills reared up behind the farmhouse. Green fields broken by low, stone walls. Thin streams of falling water. Sheer faces of black stone. High fields stretching on and on, and beyond them the peak of Mount Brandon, lost in mist. As I stood there Mr Hurley passed, following the cows. He was a quiet man with a shy smile who worked long hours in the fields with his son, so I seldom saw him. Maybe that's why I remember the things he said to me so clearly. That first day he told me about Mount Brandon. It must, he said, be treated with 'respect'. It was a practical warning about changing weather conditions on a mountain that's perilous for walkers, even in summer. But it was something else as well.

Mount Brandon's nearly two hundred million years older than the Himalayas. It's always been a place of dreams and visions. Much of the time its peak is lost in mist, pink and pale gold when the sun rises, deep gold and blood red when it sets. The only English word I know to describe it is 'numinous', a word which itself is hard to define in English; it takes in the supernatural, spiritual, divine, mysterious, fearsome and awe inspiring. The Irish word is *draíochtúil* and everyone here knows what it means. It describes Mount Brandon's blue curves edged with silver, burning against a purple sky at dusk. The moments in winter when the clouds suddenly drop and the snow-capped mountain peak blazes above them in the sun. And the contrast between the timelessness of the mountain itself and the brief human lives lived here in its presence.

On that day in Hurley's farmyard neither draíochtúil nor 'numinous' were words I knew. But I had heard stories about Mount Brandon. Irish myth and folklore are full of tales of gods and saints that inhabit high places in the landscape. They're still told in Corca Dhuibhne today, handed down through generations from the same people who built the Iron Age walls in Jack's field. In one story the sun god, Lugh, battles every year on Mount Brandon. With flashing eyes and hair and a golden spear, he strides up the mountain from the east to defeat Crom Dubh, 'the crooked, dark one'.

As a child I read that story as a fairy tale. The picture showed Lugh with hair like the rays of the sun. I coloured them in with a yellow crayon. Later on, when I studied the myth of the sun god in college, I remember sitting in the back row, doodling that image, while a dry voice lectured us about 'imagined expressions of the primeval fear of darkness.' That morning, looking up at Mount Brandon, the story of Lugh, the need to create it and the impulse to pass it on, all began to make a different kind of sense. Maybe it was because, for the first time, I'd experienced the primeval fear of darkness myself. Standing there in sunlight, watching Mr Hurley with his dog and his cows, I remembered the night before; my fearful sense in the darkness that there was no edge to anything, and then the dazzling torchlight on my face and the intense relief of knowing I wasn't alone.

There were four narrow beds in the room I'd slept in, because Mrs Hurley, like many farmers' wives on the peninsula, regularly took in students. In Ireland everyone learns Irish in school. But it's only on the west coast, in country places, that it's still the first language of the people. Along the Atlantic seaboard, in Corca Dhuibhne to the south, Connemara to the west, and Donegal to the north, there are three distinct dialects. People in the rest of the country speak English in their daily life, and school-kids pick up whichever Irish dialect their teacher happens to know. That first morning in Mrs Hurley's I remember thinking how weird it was for me to be there. Because I really should have been in Connemara.

It was chance that brought me to Corca Dhuibhne. My father was born in Galway city, on the west coast. He didn't speak Irish at home but he had family in Connemara who spoke it, so he learnt it as a child. My mother's people, from the east coast, had practically no Irish. She met and married my father in Dublin city and that's where my brothers and sisters and I were born and grew up. We spoke English at home, so what Irish I knew, I learnt at school. And it happened that my teacher spoke the dialect of Corca Dhuibhne. If I'd grown up speaking Irish with my father I'd have been sent to Connemara as a student, and maybe I'd have found my 'place of resurrection' there. I'll never know. Instead, on a dark night of stars and shifting clouds, I'd found myself on the road to Mrs Hurley's.

These days people along the Atlantic seaboard understand each other's dialects pretty well. But my neighbours here in Corca Dhuibhne remember when it was different. 'Sure none of us here knew the half of what the Connemara people were saying – or the Donegal lot either – till we got used to hearing them on the radio and the television. And that wasn't till we got the electricity!'

Getting it took time. People put electric light in the

cow-houses to begin with, then the kitchen and gradually into the bedrooms and the rest of the house. There was electricity in Mrs Hurley's on my first visit, but it had only recently been put in. On that first night the kitchen was lit by a single bulb hanging from the centre of the ceiling. But eight miles away, in the place I didn't yet know existed, there was still candlelight in Tí Neillí Mhuiris. On the morning I watched Mr Hurley and his cows. Jack, who thirty years later would become my friend, was following his own cows to pasture, having milked them by lamplight. And Neillí, whom I'd never meet, had boiled her kettle on an open fire. The bigger villages got the electricity first. Paddy was dead before his neighbours clubbed together to get mains cables brought up from the road. And Neillí, too old to live alone, had been taken to the hospital in Dingle. By that time Lís and her husband Con, who loved gardening, had become the second couple to live in Tí Neillí Mhuiris.

When I look back on my first visit to Corca Dhuibhne I seem to have done nothing but walk. These days everyone has cars. Back then there were farm carts and horses and donkeys and bikes. There were buses to Dingle, lorries and vans delivering to shops and pubs and tractors in the fields. But you could walk for miles along back roads without seeing a car or meeting another person.

You still can today. The back roads cross wide expanses of bog or lead you up between high fuchsia hedges into stony mountain fields. The fields are edged with low stone walls, and with dykes of earth. In spring and summer the hedges are alive with birdsong, watercress grows in the ditches and grey stones are lost in flowering briars and yellow lichen. The bogs are white with tall stalks of bog-cotton, moving like foam on the wind. The air smells of honeysuckle and salt.

On my first morning, slightly scared by Mr Hurley's warning, I turned my back on the high places and made my way towards the ocean. The curve of the white bay ahead of me echoed the curve of the green mountain behind. In Corca Dhuibhne three or four farms or groups of houses can make up a village. Some villages centre on a pub or a church. Others are just gatherings of farm buildings and dwellings strung along single-track roads. That morning, after a few wrong turns into muddy farmyards, I found a way between the fields and the shoreline that led to a low group of houses. One of the houses was a pub; I could see brewery barrels outside. And through the open door I could see boxes and jars behind a shop counter. It was only an hour since breakfast but, being seventeen, I needed chocolate. So I went in. It was a small room with a fire in the corner. The *bean a' tí* was behind the counter, knitting.

In Irish bean a' tí is a term both for the landlady of a

pub and a woman in her own home. It means 'woman of the house'. Places where neighbours gathered for nights of bothántaíocht were called 'rambling houses' in English. Many pubs here started life as rambling houses and went on to get a licence to sell drink. And – until new laws changed things – most pubs had a bar counter on one side and a shop counter on the other. Groceries, hardware or clothing were sold at the shop counter, or a shoemaker might sit there at his work, crossing to serve drinks from the bar when they were wanted. People came to shop, listen to music, have a pint or a cup of tea and talk with friends and strangers. Often they'd leave having forgotten what they'd come for in the first place. One pub on the outskirts of Dingle town did great business with the people from back west. 'Have you flour?' they'd say, 'and salt? Oh, and bootlaces. I was inside in Dingle for the past three hours and I never got a one of them.' I don't know the real name of that pub. It was known as *Tigh an Dearúd*, 'The House for Forgotten Things'.

Even today, pubs here are called 'houses'. In many villages back west they're almost used as extensions to people's homes. In the past, unexpected strangers could enter to a sudden silence, as if they'd invaded someone else's living room. At first they'd be met with slightly guarded curiosity and, though the welcome was always courteous, there were formalities to be observed. The pub I found that first day had packets of biscuits and bars of soap among the bottles on the shelves. On the bar counter was a teapot and a cat. As I came through the low door the bean a' tí put her knitting on her lap. I was polite. I smiled when I went in and thanked her as I left a moment later with my bar of chocolate. But, looking back now, I know she must have thought me rather rude.

It takes time to tune in to the rhythm of life here. Even now I live here myself I have to find it again each time I've been away. Manners are important. There are shared rituals everyone understands. If you pass a stranger on the road you acknowledge him. If you pass a friend you stop and talk. If you enter a shop or a business you don't start by saying what you came for. First you pass the time of day. Then you might mention the weather. If you're a local you'll exchange the latest news. One of the most common greetings among neighbours is *aon scéal*, which means 'any story?' People here work hard but there's always time for human contact. Everyone's story is important and everybody is equally worthy of attention and respect.

The ritual of saluting a stranger applies even when you're passing in a car. Whether the other person's driving or on foot, you meet his or her eye and you nod. Or raise one finger from the steering wheel as you pass. Recently, driving with Wilf in London, I discovered that remembering to retune appropriately applies in both directions. We'd slowed down in traffic when a woman stepped off the pavement to cross the road. Forgetting where I was, I automatically caught her eye and nodded as I would in Corca Dhuibhne. To anyone not used to it, the effect's rather stately and formal. The woman's eyes glazed over and she hastily changed course. I think she thought I was a weirdo who imagined I was royal.

On that first visit, when I left the pub with my bar of chocolate I followed a narrow path to the edge of a cliff. It looked west to the Blasket Islands. There at the extreme end of the peninsula the play of light between sea and sky was all around me. I walked onto the headland, a hundred feet above the Atlantic waves. The air was so pure that I could see folds in the rocks on the opposite headland, three miles away. The short grass under my feet was full of white starflowers, blue cornflowers and pink campion. The flowers were tiny, growing low to the ground and sheltered from the wind. On later visits I'd walk that way in winter when the waves were like polished pewter and the cliff was lashed by storms. But that morning, perched on a rock with my bar of Fruit & Nut, I sat in sunlight. And I remembered another of my college lectures, about the Irish sea god, Manannán Mac Lir. There's a story that describes him driving his chariot across the waves, his horses' manes tossing like white foam, and his cloak, woven of mist, changing from blue-green to silver and then to the purple of evening. Sitting at a desk in Dublin, I'd taken notes about that story. Now, sitting on a rock in Corca Dhuibhne, I watched as the wind shifted the clouds and the islands were furled in mist. Far below me, white foam curled against the cliffs. And blue-green, silver and purple waves were shining at my feet.

That evening, back at Hurley's, I dug out my college notes and settled down to read at an open window, smelling salt on the wind. What I hadn't remembered on the clifftop was that Manannán was a singer. Outside, the sun began to sink among scarlet and golden clouds. I looked up from my notes and watched, knowing that beyond the bogs and fields where Mr Hurley and his neighbours dug a living out of the earth, a pathway of light was beginning to stretch across the ocean, from the sunset to the shore.

For the people who first lived here, there was an Otherworld out there to the west. They imagined voyagers in glass boats following that path of light to a land where happiness lasts forever and a hundred years pass like a single day. I pushed the window further open and leaned out. Behind me, Mrs Hurley was humming as she worked. I could smell warm smells from her kitchen, mixed with the scent of furze on the hillside and the salt smell of the sea. The mist on the mountain was silver and pink, like the inside of a seashell.

In one of the oldest Irish stories that survives, voyagers hear singing, and out of the sea mist Manannán comes towards them, driving his chariot over the waves. And the god sings of what he sees. The voyagers think they're rowing on water but for Manannán it's a plain of flowers. For him, the leaping salmon are dancing lambs, and the glass boat floats over an orchard of fruit trees. The voyagers hear the wind but the god hears music, and the music resounds between the glory of the ocean and the high arc of the sky.

Before I came to Corca Dhuibhne I'd read about Lugh and Manannán in books. If you'd asked me then, I'd have told you I knew all about them. But I didn't. It wasn't till that first visit to Mrs Hurley's that I began to understand. Manannán, and Lugh are among the oldest gods imagined by the Celts. With Danú, goddess of fertility, they represent the numinous presence of earth, sea and sky.

When I walked home to my lunch that day I took the same road I'd walked the night before with Mr Hurley. I was thinking of the tart I'd seen Mrs Hurley put into the oven that morning, made with apples spiced with cloves. As I walked towards the farmhouse I saw a man coming from the opposite direction, pushing a bicycle. It's a straight road and I could see him from a good way off. He was a tall, dark man, wearing a cap and walking with an easy, countryman's stride. We moved towards each other along the empty road and suddenly I felt awkward. So I ducked my head as he passed, and looked away. I hadn't yet learnt about the rhythms of human contact here.

But on the same road, only moments earlier, there'd been flocks of little birds. At the sound of my feet they'd risen from the bog and whirled past in a chatter of song and a clatter of whirring wings. Then, wheeling behind their leader, streaming like a trail of smoke, they'd curved through the air to land in a field on the opposite side of the road. And I couldn't take my eyes off them.

I suppose human contact can be complex, especially when you're seventeen. And here in Corca Dhuibhne the rhythms of life were very different from those I'd been used to. But at least I'd begun to make contact with the place.

3

Kill a Calf, Kill a Cow

When I was very small I loved storytelling. I think what drew me in was the shared experience. And, above all, the expectation and satisfaction that comes from hearing again, for the second, or even the twentieth time, the rhythms and shapes of stories and sounds I'd heard before.

My grandmother lived with us in Dublin till I was four. She was my father's mother, a fearsome, sharp-eyed, formidably intelligent woman who'd ruled her own family with a rod of iron. Actually, as I write that, I'm not sure it's true. I think she may have ruled them with sulks, whims and sudden flashes of charm. One way or another, she was used to getting her own way.

I never knew my grandfather, a gentle, reclusive man who kept a barber's shop in Galway, and spent most of his time reading books instead of cutting hair. While he lived, no one challenged Granny's status or position. But when he died she suddenly found herself living in Dublin with us. It must have been hard for her. Though she adored my father, she bitterly resented my mother. I don't think it was personal. She would have seen anyone who married her son as a usurper; and now she was a dependent in the usurper's house. Always one for a dramatic gesture, as soon as she came to live with us she went straight upstairs to bed. And there she stayed, often pretending not to recognise my mother, whose days were spent running up to her with tea trays, bags of bullseyes and boiled eggs.

When Granny arrived my mother was pregnant with me. It can't have been fun balancing trays on her bump and trying to keep her temper with a mother-in-law who sat bolt upright against her pillows, demanding first look at the daily paper and yet another pot of tea. When my father came home from work and found my mother seething he used to tell her not to lose her sense of humour. Which may or may not have been helpful. I remember my mother telling me once that if ever I got angry the thing to do was to bake bread. I suspect that a good deal of the irritation from that period of her life got punched into dough. But, apparently, once I was born things got easier. Because my grandmother and I were delighted with each other. As soon as my mother brought me home I was taken upstairs and put in the crook of Granny's arm 'to keep her company'. And she used to sing to me. I don't remember the words. Only the gentle circular rhythms that used to lull me to sleep.

I don't know how far that memory goes back, and I only remember the rhythms of her songs. Words came later. I think Granny must have been a born teacher. Both my older brothers remember her encouraging them to read. As I got older she read me books as well; but what I remember most are her stories. She had silver-white hair that she plaited in two plaits and pinned across her head with white hairpins. They had to be white or they'd spoil the effect. I remember her dark eyes, a gold wedding ring, and her restless, bony hands. Sometimes she let me brush out her hair and hand her the hairpins. Other times she'd be irritated and push me away. Her stories always started the same way, 'Once upon a time, not your time and not my time but a very good time indeed . . .' They ended with a teasing chant, 'There's cakes in the oven there's cheese on the shelf, if you want any more you can sing it yourself!' Sometimes she used a more scary version, 'Kill a calf, kill a cow. There, my story's ended now!' Those are ancient formulae. Versions of them appear at the beginning and end of folktales all over the world. But when I was a child they seemed part of my grandmother's personality: beguiling, exciting, challenging and somehow faintly malicious.

Downstairs, my mother told me stories about Little Red Riding Hood and Goldilocks and the Three Bears. I loved them, but soon they seemed babyish and I was happy to move on to books. Upstairs, on granny's bed, I heard about fairy forts and fairy rings, and long, rambling stories about people she called the Too-ha-day, who lived in a starlit world beneath the hollow hills. They were full of unexplained images, of gold rings on pale, fairy fingers, and of worlds within worlds, where enchanters and shapeshifters hunted white deer with red feet, and silver birds sang on golden trees. Goldilocks and Red Riding Hood were comforting and safe. Granny's stories were different. I know now that they reach back thousands of years to the people of the goddess Danú.

Danú's name still survives in place names across Europe, from the Danube to the Don. When her people came to the Dingle peninsula they brought with them a rich and complex culture. But they didn't read or write. Everything that defined them as a people – their beliefs, customs, ideas and skills – was passed on to their children through stories, songs and poems. Now, thousands of years later, echoes of their lives are still everywhere in mine.

You hear them here in stories about Cú Chulainn, who rode into battle with his enemies' heads tied to the rim of his wicker chariot. Or of Scáthach, the warrior witch, whose name means 'The Shadowy One'. Or Níamh of the Golden Hair, in 'a dark cloak of silk down to the ground, having stars of red gold on it; her skin whiter than the swan on the wave, and her lips as sweet as honey mixed through red wine.' These stories were made to be remembered and spoken aloud. They're full of lists of words that begin with the same letter, so that one sound flows from another; and, while it was important for story-tellers to remember them accurately, there are places where people telling them added decorations of their own, like singers adding personal fireworks to a well known song.

You can tell that the Celts loved turning points, the moments of balance between one possibility and another. Their stories crackle with energy. A stag's head turns in the forest as a twig snaps under a hunter's foot. A boat hangs poised on the crest of a curling wave. You share the terror of a scream in darkness. You feel the heart-stopping moment when iron crunches into bone. The Celts' intense awareness of nature is locked into their poems, like insects suspended in amber. Their lives were shaped by the rhythmic cycle of the seasons, seed-time and harvest-time, birth, death, and rebirth. I love their humanity, vitality, and the breadth of their imagination.

They loved sex – straight, gay and bi – huge, noisy parties, grotesque humour, mind-blowing fantasy, and complex, curling patterns made in images and words.

Granny died before I went to school. So she was long dead by the time I had a eureka moment about her Too-ha-day. I was studying for an exam, listing the different places in Europe that are named after Celtic gods, when I read that Danú's name links her to place names as far apart as Denmark and Romania. On the next page there was a note about the *Tuatha Dé Danann*, the Tribe of the goddess, Danann, 'which, according to some scholars, may be another name for Danú'. In Irish *Dé* is the word for 'god'. Suddenly I made a connection. The Tuatha Dé Danann were Granny's Too-ha-day. The fairy tales I'd heard on her bed were actually stories about ancient Celtic gods.

It's not unusual for gods to dwindle into fairies. In Ireland the Tuatha Dé became a name for the pagan gods of the early settlers. As time passed and people began to worship the new, Christian god, the old gods were written off as dangerous enchanters. Eventually they dwindled even farther and became fairies living underground in fairy forts. Memories had become echoes, and the echoes were being transformed by imagination mixed with half-forgotten truths. There are fairy rings and fairy forts all round me as I write this now, sitting here at my computer in Tí Neillí Mhuiris.

The forts are the great earth-mounds that Iron Age communities piled on the graves of their dead. In stories, the graves became underground worlds. The rings are the subtle changes in colour that mark places in the landscape where the foundations of circular dwellings are present under the grass. Through centuries of imagining, these markings became places where the fairies danced at dawn, leaving dark footprints on the dew.

Half a lifetime ago, studying folklore, I learnt how people's worlds have always been shaped by their surroundings. Looking back now, I can pinpoint the first time that happened to me. I was sitting in the crook of Granny's arm. Fairy footprints on dew soaked hills come from the imagination of country people but when I first heard of fairy rings I was a city child, who hadn't yet seen dewfall. So instead of footprints on green grass, I imagined gold rings on fairy fingers. I linked them to the wedding ring on Granny's bony hand.

At university I got involved in Irish language drama. In the summers we'd tour plays around the western seaboard, a company of about a dozen of us, packed into cars with lights, sets and costumes on the roof racks, and soundboard, tents and sleeping bags in the boot. We played one-night stands in village halls and slept in fields lent by local farmers. Occasionally, we'd spend a night in a bed and breakfast, mainly so the girls in the company could wash their hair. After the show we'd go to the local pub and hear music. The instruments were traditional – fiddles, concertinas, accordions, whistles; sometimes there'd be a *bodhrán*, the traditional Irish drum, made of skin stretched on a wooden rim, and played balanced on the knee. Sometimes we'd hear stories as well. Sometimes a *sean-nós* singer would come into the pub and sit by the fire with his pint. Then we'd have a night of songs. I remember the grey light of dawn outside pub windows, turf fires sunk to glowing, grey ashes, and the music still going on.

Sean-nós means 'old custom', or 'the old way'. The songs you hear in the pubs along the Atlantic seaboard are different to the Irish folksongs sung in the cities. Sean-nós singing has roots in a time when poets and musicians did the work of modern historians, journalists and celebrity commentators. The songs are sung unaccompanied and the listeners give time-honoured murmurs of appreciation between verses. Some older singers cover their faces with their hands when they sing; often a listener holds the singer's hand during the song. There are long, formal love songs and laments, and detailed accounts of battles and loss. Other songs describe local events and characters, full of praise or malice, and sometimes both at once. Their shape and style has remained unchanged for centuries.

Each year at the end of those student tours there'd be a week in a fringe theatre in Dublin, with the luxury of real dressing rooms and sets that didn't have to go up and get taken down for every show. It wasn't long before I began working with other amateur companies. Soon I was seeing every professional show I could, first in Dublin, then in London, travelling overnight by ferry and train. By the time I finished university I'd decided I wanted to work in the theatre. Then my father died suddenly, and life was disrupted.

After that I think my confidence was shaken and I wasn't sure if I could go out and face the world. My mother was devastated by my father's death; I'm sure she'd have been happier if I'd stayed in Dublin, at least till she adjusted to her own new life without him. But she wasn't going to let me settle for something I might regret. She encouraged me to apply for a place at a London drama school and, when I was accepted, she said she'd pay my fees. So I turned down an offer of a teaching job in Dublin and took the mail boat to England, working for a summer as a chambermaid and saving to pay my living costs at drama school myself.

In London I dreamed of clouds on the mountain. On those student tours in Ireland, we'd started in the south-west and driven along the western seaboard, up through Connemara, and on to Donegal, in the north. I remember the landscape changing as we left Corca Dhuibhne and travelled through the rocky country north of Galway that my father had known as a child. It was beautiful. But

Corca Dhuibhne already had my heart. Throughout my years in university I'd kept coming back. Whenever I had a break I'd send Mrs Hurley a postcard and wait to hear if the low, whitewashed room behind her kitchen was free. If it wasn't, she'd give me the name of a neighbour and my journey over the mountain would end in another kitchen, with my feet to another fire. But the welcome was always the same. There was always strong tea and apple tart, soda bread and new-laid eggs, the whirring of wings in the hedgerows and the cows swaying heavily down long rutted lanes. At night I'd sleep deeply, aware of silence. Coming back here always felt like coming home.

So in my first months in London my dreams were of Mount Brandon. Then I'd wake in the hotel, in the stuffy room I shared with two Spanish girls, grab breakfast in a windowless kitchen and pick up my list of rooms from the housekeeper. I got making and changing beds down to a fine art, and took all the extra rooms I could get. I'd push my trolley, loaded with towels and toiletries, at double speed down the long hotel corridors. They smelt of synthetic carpets and were lit by little plastic chandeliers. As soon as you went into a room, you'd retune the bedside radio. The more up-tempo the music, the faster you got things done. The more rooms you did the more money you could save.

On my afternoon off I'd walk down New Oxford Street to a bookshop with a travel section. I remember yearning up and down the shelves, looking for books with pictures of Corca Dhuibhne. Once I found a photo of the Blasket Islands. The caption described them wallowing in the Atlantic like a grey whale with her young. I kept turning back the pages to look at it, my eyes pricking with tears. But it never occurred to me then that I could just get on the boat and go back.

Instead I went forward. I ended that summer with enough savings to pay for my time in drama school. And when I finished drama school I began my career as an actress. It's a life that needs single-minded focus, determination and drive. And buckets of luck.

First there was the quest for the holy grail. Every year a new wave of wannabees emerged from training, determined to get their hands on a union card. You couldn't work without one, so it meant months of hope, despair and bloody-minded determination not to give up trying. Most people who got lucky got their card from theatre companies. I bucked the trend and got mine through radio.

It was storytelling again. At drama school I'd loved what was called 'voice work'. Working with a microphone used all the skills I'd first heard as a child, curled up on Granny's bed, and thrilled to later in those smoky pubs along the Atlantic seaboard. The interactivity of telling and listening; eye-contact; drama; pauses full of meaning and suspense; a human voice rising and falling, beguiling, exciting, challenging. At drama school I discovered that if you get eye-contact with a microphone you can make each person out there listening think you're looking straight at them. So at the end of my last term I'd auditioned to work for BBC radio.

It was terrifying; my knees went into spasm and my tongue stuck to the roof of my mouth. But people were nice to me and I was 'put on file'. It all seemed pretty positive. Then for months nothing happened, and I joined the round of other actors just out of drama school, desperately looking for auditions, agents and Equity cards, and working in telesales and wine bars 'till something came up'. When it came up for me I was selling advertising space in newspapers. By that time I'd almost forgotten my radio audition. But someone at the BBC who'd heard my tape plucked me out of the files and offered me a job with two of the most senior actors in the business. It was the premiere of a drama by a writer whose work ranged from West End theatre to Hollywood films.

The night before I was due in the studio I put everything I'd need next day beside my bed, where I couldn't miss it. I woke about three hours early, felt too sick to eat breakfast, and set out for the station much too soon. Which was just as well, because I was standing on the platform when I realised that my script was still lying neatly by my bed. Even after a panicky gallop back to the flat, I reached the studio with an hour and a half in hand.

The play was beautifully written and its starring actors were incredibly talented, so it couldn't fail to get good notices. Because there were only the three of us, I got noticed too. It was the break that got me my union card, and my next job, which was in the theatre. Round the next bend in the road was my first job in television. I moved into a flat in Finchley with a friend from drama school. Next day I got myself a new haircut and a set of Japanese make-up brushes in a scarlet lacquer box, from South Molton Street. They cost every penny of my first television fee. But more work came along. In the excitement of the new life opening up for me, I didn't realise that each step on the road I'd chosen was leading me further away from the place that held my heart. But I don't regret it. Because it also led me to Wilf.

We met in the theatre in London, where he was working as an opera director. He'd been to Ireland more recently than I had because he'd done a show there, at the Wexford Opera Festival. Wexford was my mother's county, on the east coast. When I met him, Wilf had never been to the west. I hadn't been there myself for several years. Whenever I had time and money I went to Dublin, where my family was. It never seemed possible to keep going all the way across Ireland, over the mountain to Dingle and on back west. In those days, anything more than a snatched break from my career felt dangerous. I was always afraid that I'd lose my focus, and fail.

Wilf was born in Hertford, just outside London. He was a few years ahead of me in his own career, already doing shows in the West End. He and his brother, James, grew up with music. James became a conductor. Wilf became a theatre director, in musicals and opera. I wasn't particularly impressed. I'd had piano lessons as a child but I was useless at it and sulked and complained till I was allowed to give them up. So when Wilf and I met I'd hardly been to a classical concert, and never to an opera. He took me to Mozart's *Marriage of Figaro* at the English National Opera, conducted by James. It was nothing like any music I'd heard before. Though when the Countess sang about her love-rat husband at the beginning of the second act, I recognised the same intensity of loss I'd heard in sean-nós songs. Later, when I'd heard more of Wilf's music, I wondered how he'd react to a bunch of fiddles and flutes and concertinas in a smoky pub back west. I never imagined that twenty years later he'd be playing a concertina here himself.

We came to Corca Dhuibhne on our honeymoon. We hired a car and drove from Dublin to Donegal, on down the western seaboard through Connemara and Galway, out along the Dingle peninsula and over the Conor Pass into the west. The road over the pass has been widened since then. But even now there are places where I have to hold my breath. On that first trip, as we crawled between a bulging rock and a sheer drop, Wilf was concentrating on his driving. I was concentrating on not thinking about the drop. Then, as a car approached us from above, we pulled in to a passing place and had time to look around. Beside us a narrow torrent of water streamed down the rock face, under the road, and into the valley below. Miles away across the valley, down the sheer eastern face of Mount Brandon, were other silver strips of falling water. Below us were three lakes, flat as beaten metal. Around them were green fields, bounded by stone walls. Shadows of high clouds were drifting over the landscape. The car coming towards us passed us by. The road curved with the contours of the mountain as we sidled on upwards, Wilf pretending not to be bothered and me still holding my breath. At the top, I breathed out carefully. Then I looked at Wilf's face. The weather was perfect. Below us was the tapering end of the peninsula, surrounded by the vast expanse of the Atlantic Ocean, flecked with silver foam. I had a sudden vision of Manannán's horses tossing their manes. Farther out to sea the waves were shimmering emerald, turquoise and pale jade, their colours constantly changed by the shadows of the clouds. We sat there for a long moment, grinning at each other like idiots. Then Wilf put the car into gear, and we drove down the far side of the mountain, up the steep streets of Dingle town, and out back west.

In the years since I'd last been there, one of Mrs Hurley's sons, Máirtín, had built a fine new bungalow for guests beside the family house. But her rooms were all booked, so we'd decided to stay a few nights here and there in different B&Bs. Nothing had changed. We were welcomed with open hands and gentle greetings. We had new-laid eggs and soda bread for breakfast, and drank strong tea by turf fires. Wilf developed a taste for cloves in apple pies. Our days were spent walking long, empty beaches and driving down long, winding roads. There was hogweed on the ditches, and long tendrils of briar curling round vivid green ferns.

One day, out driving, we heard bleating and found a sheep struggling in a bog. Only her head was visible above the wet, black mud that was dragging her down. We'd no idea what to do. Eventually we drove on to the nearest farmhouse, where a man in stained jeans and muddy boots was working in the yard. He listened to our story, swung into a jeep without a word and let out a piercing whistle. As the jeep turned onto the road a sheep dog shot out of the barn, leapt a stone wall and landed in the back. Driving back to our B&B, we passed the bog again.

The dog was poised, quivering, in the jeep, while the man, who'd roped the sheep, was about to drag her out. He raised one hand to us, caked with dripping, black mud. We waved back and drove on.

That night our bean a' tí discovered that Wilf's a musician and sent us down the local pub. 'It should be a good session. They've just been playing in New York.' But when we arrived it was packed. Local fishermen in smelly oilskins jostled with guys from a Dublin record company and the music was practically inaudible in the scrum. We'd just decided to give up and go when one of the musicians turned his head and saw us across the crowd. Suddenly he grinned and waved, people shuffled out of the way, and we were bundled to the front and presented with pints. Perched on the best seats in the house, we sat enthralled as the musician's flying fingers led the other players into a set of reels. He'd changed out of his work boots and jeans. But his fingers were still stained by the black mud from which he'd rescued his sheep. It was our first introduction to the many-sided lives that people live here.

I watched Wilf that night as he followed the rhythms of the music. Like me he was loving it. But, being a musician, he was also following its mathematical sequences. You could practically see the wheels turning in his brain, and I knew he was hooked. The next day, sitting on warm stones, eating apples, I told him about Granny's songs and he remembered his own grandmother, who'd died when he was eight. As she got older, she'd retreated into a quiet world of her own, peopled with images from her childhood. She didn't talk much, but she loved listening to music. He remembers playing the piano to her when he was a child. Sometimes she'd have conversations with people he couldn't see. She didn't sing to him, but she smiled and beat time when he played the tunes of her favourite hymns.

That day in Corca Dhuibhne was one of those lazy days when you talk of everything and nothing. I suppose Wilf was remembering the session we'd been to the night before when, in the middle of the story about his own grandmother, he asked if my Galway granny was a sean-nós singer. When I'd finished choking on my apple, I told him she wasn't.

In Granny's world, wearing a shawl and speaking Irish made you a peasant, while a hat and coat and a command of English made you a cut above the rest. There's a family story about the day she was walking down Shop Street in Galway, 'thinking about something' when a barefoot shawlie woman came towards her from the opposite direction. In a moment of aberration, wearing her good hat and her decent cloth coat, Granny stepped into the gutter and 'gave the shawlie woman the flags', or flagstones, that made up the pavement. Apparently she was so mortified she went straight home, got into bed and refused to get up again. It was obviously her default position when life went horribly wrong.

That's why Wilf's innocent question made me choke. Then, and for years afterwards, it never even occurred to me that Granny might have known Irish. But when I started writing this book, my brother told me she'd told him she used to speak it to the Connemara men who came into the barber's shop in Galway. Now I wonder if she spoke it herself as a child. Her stories of the Too-ha-day were told to me in English. But the rhythms and turns of phrase she used in them didn't belong to her ordinary conversation. They came straight from the Irish language. Was that how she'd first heard them herself? I'll never know the answer. That memory's been lost forever. But I do know that somehow, despite her coat and hat, Granny had inherited the shawlie women's tradition. I wish she hadn't lived in a world that taught her to be ashamed of it.

I have no family roots in Corca Dhuibhne. But here in this house of memories there are echoes of Granny's songs. Neillí Mhuiris and her neighbours here had work songs that went with their daily chores, like spinning and milking, making bread and rocking the baby to sleep. Women here still remember them and pass them on from mother to daughter, even though working days here now are more likely to be spent at a computer. They were little, rhythmic, circular tunes, made to fit the beat of the repetitive tasks that made up daily life here for centuries. Listening to them today, I remember sitting curled in the crook of my fearsome granny's arm. She used the same circular rhythms to lull me to sleep on her bed.

4

Circles

'It was a dark and stormy night. And the rain came down in torrents. And the farmer said to his son, John, "John! Draw down to the fire and I'll tell you a story." So John drew down to the fire. And the farmer went on as follows. "It was a dark and stormy night. And the rain came down in torrents. And the farmer said to his son, John, "John! Draw down to the fire and I'll tell you a story." So John drew down to the fire. And the farmer went on as follows . . ."' (Long pause. My father was a master of suspense. Then a deep breath, and off he'd go again.) 'It was a dark and stormy NIGHT. And the rain came down in TORRENTS. And the farmer said to his son, JOHN, "JOHN! Draw down to the fire and I'll tell you a story."' But by that stage I'd have taken myself upstairs, and put myself to bed. Which was exactly what my father had intended.

Each night when I was small he'd read aloud to me at bedtime, sitting by the fire. I remember copies of *Swiss Family Robinson* and *Alice In Wonderland* with dates pencilled in the margins to show where we'd got to each night, the smell of the pages, the rubbed red cloth bindings and the dark, slightly scary wood engravings in *Alice*. It was a nightly ritual with a comforting, rhythmic shape of its own. If I begged for more when the reading was over, my father always shut the book and shook his head. And if I kept pleading, half dreading and half inviting the next stage in the ritual, he'd always begin the same teasing, circular chant about the storytelling farmer and his son.

I never saw that story written down but, in my mind, I linked it to a book I'd got from my godfather on my birthday. It was a beautifully produced, illustrated collection of *Tales from the Arabian Nights*, as big as a broadsheet newspaper, with a creamy grey hardback cover, stamped in gilt with repeated oriental patterns. The people in the *Arabian Nights* were caliphs and viziers who lived in palaces, while John and his storytelling dad lived in an Irish farmhouse, but the idea of stories within stories, told night after night by the Sultan's wife to ward off her death, gave me the same pleasure I found in the circular rhythms of my father's chanted story about the dark and stormy night. I read recently that the opening line of that story came from a Victorian novel. But the tradition of circular stories and tales within tales is ancient, and worldwide, reaching back before stories were ever written down. The Celts loved them. They chimed with their vision of life as an endlessly turning wheel. And the repeated patterns and circular rhythms in Celtic storytelling, and the circles and spirals carved on the standing stones they raised here in Corca Dhuibhne, are images of their vision of eternity.

Corca Dhuibhne became the place that Wilf and I would escape to. I'd started writing as well as acting, beginning with radio scripts and children's TV, and moving on to soap opera. Meanwhile, Wilf was working long hours on actual operas at Covent Garden. At the same time I was fitting in voice work; one day it'd be a commercial, next day a training programme, or a film. Rushing from tube stations to sound studios, and then back to my desk to grab something to eat before concentrating on the next deadline, I'd imagine days spent wandering rutted back roads, and cups of tea served by turf fires with slabs of buttered soda bread.

Whenever we could, we'd make a dash for Dingle. Once we'd hit the peninsula, our first stop was at a place called Inch. The floor of Sammy's café there was powdered with windblown sand, and the air outside was alive with sea birds. It's been rebuilt since, but then Sammy's was hardly more than a low shed by the beach. We'd have tea and apple cake at the open window, looking out at the curve of the bay and along miles of empty beach and rolling sand dunes. Then we'd drive on, over the mountain, to long, relaxing days and quiet nights.

At some point on one of those visits we passed Tí Neillí Mhuiris. I don't remember it but Wilf does. We'd driven over the high pass called the Clasach that leads up from the village of Dún Chaoin, at the extreme end of the peninsula. The road rises between the last two peaks of Corca Dhuibhne's mountain spine. As you climb it, you can look back and see the Blasket Islands, three miles out into the ocean. There's a story about an islandwoman who crossed the Blasket Sound to Dún Chaoin, and set out to cross the Clasach. As she reached the top of the pass she looked back at her island, half hidden in mist, far below her. Then she looked ahead to where the road ran down between the mountains and into the valley below. Behind her, and in front, the ocean stretched to the horizon. And the road was dusty under her feet. 'Oh what a wide place the world is!' she said. And she went back to her island, and never left it again.

The day Wilf and I drove over the Clasach we were going nowhere in particular. He remembers fine, windy weather, and stopping now and then to take photos. The narrower and more overgrown a road is, the more likely Wilf is to follow it. We'd driven down several tracks that day, and had to reverse the car out of fields and farmyards. Coming down from the Clasach we'd paused and doubled back so often that I'd given up wondering where we were. But Wilf remembers turning down the road that now leads us to our own front gate.

It's a steep hill, running between walls of scarlet fuchsia growing on high banks of earth and stone. At the first turn in the road, we would have passed the gate. Biddy, the nurse, probably lived there then. But the hedge was high, so if we'd looked in that day we'd have seen nothing but the gable end, and a glimpse of Paddy's ash trees. Anyway, Wilf was probably concentrating on his driving. He remembers slowing down as we turned the corner by Jack's farm. There were dogs outside the row of low, stone sheds, and milk churns on the concrete stand by the roadside. The sheds' roofs were painted in black tar. A red hen was pecking at watercress by a shallow stream. Jack's single-storeyed house, on the right, looked just as it does today. Across a yard was a high cowshed, roofed in corrugated iron, with a haybarn behind it. Across the road, on the left, was Manning's farm, a two-storey house with its farm buildings behind it. Neither of us remembers seeing Jack that day. He was probably in the fields, or out of sight, tinkering with his tractor. But, more than twenty years later, as I type this, I can see him now through my window. He's walked up the road with his dogs to help Wilf earth up the potatoes.

Our favourite café back west was in Dún Chaoin. We found it on one of our first trips here, when we took the spectacular drive round Slea Head, at the end of the peninsula. It was a sunny day in Maytime. The Slea Head drive snakes round the westernmost cliffs, every turn revealing a new view of the Blasket Islands. The steep fields, bounded by drystone walls, run straight down to the edge of the cliffs. Round one corner the road disappears into a shallow stream, and we splashed through it, our tyres scrunching on rolling pebbles. At the farthest end of the peninsula we parked, scrambled over a wall by the road, and joined three seagulls in a field that was almost perpendicular. Out on the Great Blasket, which people here just call 'the island', we could see sand gleaming on a beach they call 'the white strand'. *Inis Tuaisceart*, 'the northern island', is known as 'The Dead Man'. Its rocky outline floating on the ocean looks exactly like a corpse laid out for burial. Though these days, when it's pointed out to tourists, it's sometimes called 'The Sleeping Giant'. Death's not a subject that goes down too well with holidaymakers.

As Wilf and I sat there, I remembered stories of the islanders dancing on the white strand in Maytime. No one lives on the islands now, but in the past they'd gather on the strand to celebrate festivals and holidays. There are photos of dances on the white strand when summer visitors came to the island in the 1920s. In the past, in some parishes on the mainland, people would walk miles to dance in the open air to the music of fiddles at crossroads. If there was no musician they'd make 'mouth music', singing the wordless rhythms of the dance. Jack's generation here remembers a life of hard work and poverty. His sister Máirín told me how, as a child, she used to worry about her father's cows. 'We depended on them. And if they died we had nothing. Your living that year would be gone.' That's a phrase people here use a lot. 'We had nothing,' they say, 'less than nothing.' There were times when they were hungry. They worked backbreaking hours on the farms. But, even so, they had nights and days full of music and dancing.

It was a life in which each season followed the next with its allotted work and traditional customs. In Maytime, all over Ireland, people used to bring wildflowers or green branches indoors, to welcome and encourage new growth in the fields. Country people in England had the same custom. Hertford, Wilf's family home, is now almost a suburb of London, but when his mother was born it was still part of the countryside.

I knew she loved wild flowers; she used to point them out on country walks and we have a page of flowers she painted in watercolours. She signed it in the bottom right-hand corner with a little picture of a bird. Somewhere I'd seen photos of Maypoles and Hertfordshire children carrying garlands so, as we sat in the cliff field looking at the islands, I asked Wilf if his mum had memories of May Day celebrations when she was a child. But if she had, she never passed them on.

In Irish, *Bealtaine* is the word for May. It's also the name of one of four, seasonal festivals. Traditionally, the year here starts in winter, not spring, affirming that life comes from darkness, and everything begins with a dormant seed. Each festival takes place at a turning point in the year. The people who lived in the Iron Age dwelling in Jack's field measured their lives by those turning points. So did Neillí and Paddy. They celebrated them with traditional food, music and dancing. So do people who live here today.

The Celts' festival of *Samhain* began in November; *Imbolc*, in February; *Bealtaine*, in May; and *Lughnasa*, in August. They were communal feasts, ritual responses to seed time and harvest time, darkness and light. Each festival had its own dances, music, customs and food. In lots of places in Ireland they've recently been revived as food, music, art and film festivals. But, at heart, they're expressions of ordinary communities' hopes and fears for their families, harvests, and animals. Back west in Corca Dhuibhne, they've always shaped people's lives. That day, when Wilf and I climbed out of the cliff field and got back in the car, we drove on round Slea Head towards Dún Chaoin. As we went, I repeated the names of the festivals, and laughed at his attempts to pronounce them. We'd no idea then that, twenty years later, they'd shape our lives as well.

The Dún Chaoin café's in a pottery and bookshop run by two sisters. Among the books and pots are piles of handknitted sweaters and cardigans, smelling faintly of oiled wool. As you lift the latch on the half door that separates the shop from the café, you're met by the smell of baking. There's a collection of delicate china on two wooden dressers, old jugs, pink and white gilded cups and painted souvenir plates; visitors often try to buy them but they're not for sale. The café's the most westerly eating place in Europe and its tables look out on the islands. You can carry your tray outside, to a low, stone wall or a wooden table, and eat watching seals diving, or – if you're lucky – basking sharks. On the day Wilf and I first found it, we sat out in the sun and ate black porter cake and plates of rhubarb tart with yellow cream.

In those years, because our breaks were precious, I remember always hoping for sunshine and feeling slightly cheated if it rained. The weather here is unpredictable; it's said you can experience the four seasons in one day.

But after an exhausting period in London we felt we deserved the sun. It seemed like we'd worked for it. Now, years later, I recognise the frustrated look of visitors hunched in anoraks, glowering at the weather. My neighbours here who run guest houses are used to anxious questions over breakfast. 'Do you think it will rain?' 'Is it going to dry up?' 'If the wind drops do you think we'll get over to the island?' The answer to all those questions is 'maybe'. Or *n'fheadair*, which means 'I don't know'. People who live here are good at reading the weather. But they're used to working with it, not against it. If the wind and sea are rising, you don't take out a boat. If the day's too wet for digging, there's no point in setting out for the field; you'll only break your back and spoil the ground for tomorrow. Of course, a cow calves when her time comes, rain or shine. But, where they can, people suit their work to the weather, and it all gets done in the end. '*Ní hé lá na gaoithe lá na scoilbe*,' they say. 'The windy day is not the day for thatching.' They take things as they come. It's not an attitude that sits well with the idea that hard work and determination will deliver whatever you want. But here it's just logical. No amount of determination can stop the rain. And why would you want to, anyway? Without rain, nothing grows.

In London I'd started to weave stories from Corca Dhuibhne's legends and folklore into the scripts I wrote for the BBC. Then, sitting in front of a microphone, I'd conjure up the place I most wanted to be. Kings and warriors hunted the slopes I'd climbed above Hurley's farm. In my mind's eye queens and poets sailed boats round rocky headlands. Remembering carved stones in high fields, I'd imagine entrance points to Granny's fairy forts, and call up enchanted armies from stalks of grass and the tops of the watercress, from ragwort, and from withered leaves. Deep in the twilight world of the Tuatha Dé, they rode in chariots of white bronze ribbed with silver. They wore purple cloaks and silk coats, fastened with hooks of gold, furled close to their white bodies. Their bull-hide shields had silver rims, studded with amber. In front of each rider crouched a driver, urging the horses on with silver flails. I saw their eyes, wide, grey and shining; and their white teeth, pointed like the teeth of hounds.

Afterwards I'd emerge from Broadcasting House into Oxford Street and join the crowds of commuters flooding down to the underground stations after the working day. Sitting on the train, with my head against the window, I'd watch the signs on the platforms as the train clattered from dark tunnels through lighted stations. For a moment they'd flash past the window; Earl's Court, West Kensington, Gunnersbury. And in my mind's eye I'd see different place names; The Fort Of The Cats, The Hawk's Bay, The Eagle's Mountain, The Hag's Valley, The Road Of Stones.

As well as working, and snatching breaks in Corca Dhuibhne, Wilf and I had found our first home together. It was a maisonette in a west London suburb. We bought it before property prices went crazy and did it up ourselves, squeezing the work into our already over-crowded lives. It was an upstairs flat in a terrace. An outside staircase led down to a tiny, shared backyard, with a coal bunker and two washing lines. On one side of the yard was a small, sad flowerbed. That was ours. On the other side, about two steps away, was a slightly larger one. It was dominated by a garden shed, bizarrely plonked in the middle of it, standing on breeze blocks. That belonged to May, our downstairs neighbour. She also had a strip of concrete path, bordered by a narrow flowerbed that led to her back door.

I met May in the yard on our first day in the flat. As a student I'd been used to flats where we never knew the neighbours. Later, working in theatre and television, the places I lived were really just places to crash after an exhausting day's work. So meeting May was my first introduction to living in a London neighbourhood. When she introduced herself, she told me that the longer and higher of the washing lines belonged to us, but that she'd always had the use of it for her big wash on Wednesdays, 'by arrangement'. We agreed that the arrangement should stand. Then she added sadly that the shed in the middle of her flowerbed was ours too. Apparently it had belonged to Rose, who'd lived in our flat and had installed the shed on the flowerbed one day while May was out. 'She didn't want it on her own side, you see. So she had it put on mine while my back was turned. It was a lock-up for her motorbike.'

May was a tiny widow in her eighties, and I was horrified to hear how she'd been treated. I imagined some aggressive, tattooed biker, roaring down motorways at weekends with a pack of leather clad Hell's Angels. I nodded sympathetically, and May leant on the coal bunker. 'Rose was a difficult girl, you know. And a dreadful bully at school.' By this stage I could see Rose as the neighbour from hell, an abusive, leering teenager, thumping about over a defenceless pensioner's head. 'Anyway,' said May, perking up suddenly, 'I just wanted to say that the shed's yours by rights. It goes with your flat.' I protested, but she shook her head. 'If your husband's a gardener he'll find it useful.' She looked at the two tiny flowerbeds. 'There's a lot here wants looking after.' She was halfway to her door when she looked round again, anxiously. 'I hope Rose doesn't decide to come back.' 'I'm sure she won't,' I said kindly, feeling rather anxious myself, 'where has she moved to?' 'Sri Lanka.' I felt relieved. Return from Sri Lanka seemed unlikely. May mistook my relief for surprise. 'I know,' she said, 'I told her it was daft at her age. I said to her, at eighty-five, if a snake bites you, you're done for. But she wouldn't listen. She never did.'

We were half expecting to find a Harley-Davidson in the garden shed, but it was empty. We heard later that, before leaving for Sri Lanka, Rose had sold her bike to 'some chap down the pub'. So Wilf used the shed to store his tools. He grew up in a house with a garden and open fields close by, so for him any patch of earth, however small or unpromising, is a project. When he wasn't spending evenings and weekends wallpaper stripping, laying floors, and wiring in the flat, he took over the two flowerbeds and covered the outside staircase and its railings with boxes and pots. We had morning glories and evening primroses, herbs and a bay tree; and the crimson peony in May's flowerbed was pruned and mulched and given a new lease of life. It was in that tiny space that a new sense of the passing seasons first entered my London life.

Wherever you are in the western hemisphere, there's a moment each year when the sap rises, and winter turns to spring. Farmers and gardeners can feel it under their hands; but everyone instinctively responds to it, even if we don't know why. It's the impulse that ad agencies play on when they tell us to dump our granite work surfaces and have a spring makeover in yellow Corian. It's what makes us wrinkle our noses at black trousers and start thinking about floaty floral prints. In our first home Wilf and I took pleasure in the return of our morning glories and the scent of May's lily-of-the-valley. We drove to the garden centre on spring bank holiday and joined the scrum buying bedding plants and garden chairs. But even so, my life was still focused on work so most of its pleasures were either snatched or deferred. Besides, I lived in a world where spring flowers can be bought the whole year round.

For thousands of years, the Celts celebrated the cycle of the seasons as a sign that the universe was in balance. In their world view, everything that lives must die to live again; so life and death have equally vital places in a repeated pattern, expressed by the seasons of the year. And in the Celts' circular image of eternity each thing follows the next in its allotted sequence, like the notes of a tune or the steps in a dance.

But for us in the twenty-first century, life's a straight line. Each year, at school, at work, in everything we strive for, we're encouraged to look back and see how far we've come – and then we're told to keep forging ahead. But, as we do, we're desperate to avoid what's down the line. We fear ageing so much that our ideal female bodies are prepubescent. We pay to have poison injected into our faces and our highest hope is that one day, somehow, scientists will discover a way to eliminate death. It's a far cry from the Celts' belief that ageing was ripening and death was full of hope.

After we'd been a few months in the flat, Kath, the elderly lady next door, asked Wilf to take down the fence separating our yard from hers, so her plants would get more light. Her yellow climbing rose responded with a spurt of growth, and her son, who looked after her garden, had to come and tie it back to its trellis. Wilf and I would sit out by the dustbins with a bottle of wine, watching the evening primroses' pale yellow trumpets spiral open in the last of the sunlight and glow like lanterns in the dusk. But in winter, when everything died back, the concrete got slimy with green mould. The place where we'd sat on summer evenings reverted to a dank space for the bins. And then, the following spring, self seeded morning glories began to show. Along the pathway to May's back door, a mass of lily-of-the-valley flourished in the shade, scenting the whole yard, and gleaming like dim pearls. May looked at them as if they were stray cats. 'They come back the same time every year, I don't know why. They were here before my time, I do know that.'

We still kept escaping across the Irish Sea and over the mountain to Corca Dhuibhne. After months of cosseting pot plants in a concrete yard, the lushness here was intoxicating. Grants from the European Union have widened and straightened the roads nearest the sea, used by tourist coaches. But each year, on the back roads, strips of grass force their way through tarred surfaces, seeded by birds and the droppings of cattle and sheep. In summer, the earth and stone walls by the roadsides disappear under miles of scarlet fuchsia bushes and montbretia, a slender, orange lily with neon green leaves. Fuchsia and mont-bretia are outsiders, escapees from gardens; they thrive in Corca Dhuibhne's climate. Among them grow older plants, briars and ferns, cow parsley and valerian, tiny purple orchids and powder blue cornflowers; Wilf and I used to walk roads, arguing about their names. I was trying to remember in two languages, which didn't help. At one point he accused me of only knowing the name for nettles. I pointed out that nettles aren't to be sneered at – they're a powerful herb that the old people here used to ease the pains of rheumatism.

We'd bicker on lazily till it'd start to drizzle, and then we'd sit in the car, waiting for rainbows. When you learn to relax there's pleasure in Corca Dhuibhne's changing weather. A house down the road can be lost in mist while you're standing in sunshine. You can watch rain coming towards you on the wind. The peninsula's in the same time zone as London, but the summer evenings here are longer. In June and July we could still see honeysuckle and meadowsweet shining by the roadsides at midnight.

In the first years of our marriage, winter breaks here weren't easy. Most B&Bs closed after the summer season. I remember travelling over from London in October once, when we stayed in Dingle. We'd chucked things in a bag and set off at a moment's notice, escaping some major irritation at work that I've now forgotten. Like bees making for a hive, we drove straight to Dún Chaoin. The pottery café was open and one of the two sisters was working in the kitchen. She was wearing an apron over a heavy, handknitted cardigan, like the ones for sale in her shop. We ordered tea and porter cake and, determined to recapture a sense of holiday relaxation, asked if we could take the tray outside. There was a flicker of astonishment. But people here are always courteous. She held the door for us as we carried out the tray. Outside, wrapped in scarves, coats and hats, we sat in an Atlantic gale, attempting to eat porter cake wearing gloves. Below on the cliffs, the waves threw strips of foam high into the fields. But we were determined. I grasped the teapot, Wilf held out his cup, and I poured the tea. There was a violent gust of wind and the stream of boiling liquid shot sideways from the spout, missing Wilf by inches. Moments later, exactly the same thing happened when I tried to pour the milk. At that point we gave up and went inside. Our hostess, warm in her woolly cardigan, was too polite to comment.

In winter, when days are short, the landscape here changes. Atlantic storms drive in from north and west. Colour leaches from the mountains. As summer growth dies back, the hard shapes of the roadside walls reappear, and neon green, scarlet and orange become soft greys and umbers. The sky's reflection in the ocean changes from turquoise to pewter. When you walk on the naked mountains, the wind drives you backwards like a punch in the gut, scooping your breath out and scouring your skin. And the waves' strength is terrifying; only a few years ago, during a winter gale, a whole section of road crashed into the sea at Dún Chaoin. Rain can fall for weeks on end and, as the weight of water increases, rivers flood. Sheep are blown over the cliffs. Regularly, climbers who ignore the locals' warnings have to be rescued from the mountains. Sometimes, the rescuers find them too late.

But if you only know Corca Dhuibhne in summer, you miss half of what it can teach you. It's in the turn of the year's wheel, from darkness to light and back again to darkness, that you recognise your own small place in a larger picture. I didn't know that when I was just a visitor here. I know it now.

As I sit here writing this, I'm remembering the first winter Wilf and I spent here in Tí Neillí Mhuiris. One day in January we went for a walk after a night of violent storms. Coming back, we found trails of seaweed on the road to the house, a good two miles from the sea. By then we'd heard the story of Paddy's fear of the wind, and the neighbours had warned us to pile stones on anything we left outdoors in winter. But could wind and waves really hurl seaweed two miles inland? Then, as we turned through the gate, we found a huge mound of the dripping weed, waist high, standing in the middle of the garden. Baffled, we went indoors to shed our coats and pile turf on the fire. It was hours later that Jim George, our neighbour from up the mountain, dropped by, and the mystery was solved. Every year, for longer than anyone can remember, people on this mountain have waited for the particular storms that cover the nearest beaches with seaweed. Each year the storms come, the call goes out, and people make their way to the shore. While we'd been out walking, Jim had been out with a pitchfork gathering weed. On his way home he'd dropped some in for us. 'You'll want it now in the next week or two,' he said. We were touched but still baffled. Why would we want seaweed? There was an agonising moment when Jim was probably too polite to notice our ignorance and we were certainly too embarrassed to admit it. Then the penny dropped. The cycle of the year had turned. It was time to start preparing the land for planting. Once again, the sea had delivered the means of fertilising the earth. And because Jim's brother Mike has a tractor and we haven't, Jim had done the neighbourly thing and hauled us up a share.

For years, Wilf and I used Corca Dhuibhne as a place where we snatched pleasure and relaxation. But in Tí Neillí Mhuiris I've begun to understand what happens when you live your life in a community, to the rhythm of the seasons. Nothing need be snatched at, or deferred.

Instead, each moment's savoured as it comes. Nothing's missed. And everything's shared.

As soon as we'd bought the London flat, we snatched a weekend here in Corca Dhuibhne. We wanted to cross from Dún Chaoin to the island. I forget where we were staying, but I remember eating breakfast with one eye on the weather, and driving to Dún Chaoin hoping that the ferry would sail. You walk to the pier down a steep slipway, part path and part steps. It turns sharply as it spirals down the side of the cliff. The wall's partly concrete, partly jagged outcrops of rock. As you reach the bottom, you can see the remains of a narrower, even steeper, path, used by the fishermen before the current one was built. It's hard to believe they climbed it carrying their nets and their catch.

When we got to the island we had to transfer from the ferry to a rubber dinghy. I told myself firmly that the islanders had rowed that way with nothing but timber spars and tarred canvas between their braced feet and the heaving ocean. But the dinghy seemed awfully close to the waves. So I fixed my eyes on a gannet circling on an upcurrent of air and tried not to think about rocks. Then I realised we'd cleared a breakwater and were coming alongside a slipway. I jumped, landed on the slipway and moved on, making way for the others, jumping out behind me. The way ahead was a narrow, curving path up a cliff.

There's a black-and-white photo, taken in 1910 when the island slipway was built. It shows a group of islandmen with long-handled shovels posing rather self-consciously for the camera. They're wearing boots or shoes, trousers held up by braces, heavy woollen sweaters or jackets, and hats or caps. Among them is a young man with bare feet and a bare head. He's a visiting English academic, unsuitably dressed for the job but mucking in happily, with a huge smile on his face. It's a picture of a *meitheal*.

In Irish, meitheal is the word for a group of neighbours who come together to help on a job that can't be done by a single family. I remember sitting in Gorman's once when Síle recalled a meitheal at harvest time on Vincent's family farm. 'You wouldn't believe it,' she said, 'his mother would cook on an open fire and feed twenty men.' Then, when the work was done, the same men would move on and help the next neighbour, working their way round the parish until everyone's harvest was in.

That day on the island, Wilf and I climbed from the slipway to the steep, grassy road leading to the ruined village, a group of abandoned houses clustered against the wind. High above them, at the edge of a dizzying cliff, we lay on cushions of sea-pink. Far below us was the luminous white strand. The sea round the islands was a dazzling silver sheet. With the sun high in the sky it seemed impossible to believe in days and nights of darkness and howling wind. But the islanders lived a precarious life, cut off from the mainland for weeks at a time in winter. Often they were close to starvation, and to make a living from the unpredictable ocean and their salty fields they had had no choice but to work together as a community. Without the tradition of the meitheal they couldn't have survived.

In 1936, when her community was slowly being lost to emigration, a Blasket islandwoman called Peig Sayers dictated a book to her son. It's called *Peig*, and it's the story of her life. Peig married in from the mainland, where she'd grown up listening to her father's stories. She brought them with her into the island, and told them at evenings of bothántaíocht, when people came together in each others' houses after their day's work. One island house was known as the *dáil*, or parliament, because when newspapers came from the mainland the men used to sit there and discuss the ways of the world. The island-women had their own particular places to chat and share stories; but their discussions about childbirth, sex, bad hair days and relationships were never shared with men. So those particularly female memories didn't make it into Peig's books. They died with her and her neighbours who chatted round the well and in the fields. Talking about it now, my own neighbours here will shake their heads. 'It was men who wrote things down and came and recorded things. So the women's memories were lost.'

When I was at school we had to read Peig's book for an exam. And we hated it. I remember being told she'd wanted to pass on to us what she'd learned from her own life. Her photo's on the cover – a picture of a wrinkled old woman in a black shawl, looking into the camera with weather-creased eyes. Then, I couldn't imagine that life had taught her anything I'd ever need. Now when I look at her face I can see shrewdness and serenity, resilience, and the wisdom of old age. And I grieve for those lost memories.

In London, May and Kath were wonderful neighbours; and they were the first friends I made as an adult from a generation older than my own. May's only daughter was in Australia, so May lived alone. Once a week, she and a friend went out dancing. 'It's a club, love, for pensioners, they've got a little bar, and a tea place, and music. No men, mind, near as makes no difference, but we get around the floor.' On dry Wednesday afternoons, she'd hang out her 'big wash' for the week; Wilf had fixed the pulley on the high washing line in the yard, 'which was a load off my mind, love, what with the weight of my sheets.' As soon as her two single sheets, her towels and her nightie were flapping on the line, she'd walk round the corner to pick up her friend. Then, with their dancing shoes in supermarket carrier bags, they'd walk on to the end of the road, and catch the bus. Once, they got a bit worried because a man seemed to be following them, 'but we tipped the wink to the bus driver, and he shut the door on him.' Then, one Wednesday, I noticed she hadn't gone out and I asked if her friend wasn't well. 'Oh, she's fine love, but they've stopped the dancing. Council can't afford it. Shame, really. Those shoes I have indoors got years of dancing left in them.'

The flat gave us our first experience of designing and creating a space where we could live and work. Looking back now, I realise how much May and Kath had to put up with from our DIY. I apologised to May once, after a weekend of drilling over her head. She just shrugged. 'Never mind, love, it's all got to be done.' Kath was just as kind but slightly more ironic when Wilf told her he'd finished working on the kitchen walls. 'I thought you had. Tongue and groove boards, is it?' It was, and she must have heard each nail that went into every one of them. Later she came up to inspect the works. When she saw we'd opened up the fireplace in the front room she gave us a brass-topped poker. 'I don't need it, dear, I use gas.' I was touched by her gift, especially when I found it was made by her husband, Walter. He'd cut and filed the thread on the steel shaft himself, and the brass knob on top, worn by years of use, was a carefully chosen door handle.

Walter had died the year before we moved into our flat and Kath missed him dreadfully. She and I used to sit in the yard and talk about her climbing rose, our morning glories, and May's lily-of-the-valley. But at the time her raw sorrow made me feel awkward, so we never talked about that. Now I wish we had. Because I think that, for Kath, death was full of hope. The day she discovered that Wilf was an opera director her eyes filled with tears; she and Walter had loved listening to recordings, but they'd never been to an opera. Later that year Wilf took her to a performance at Covent Garden. In the second interval he had to go backstage and while he was there, he mentioned Kath. He came back to his seat with a message for her from the tenor, who'd said he'd sing his next aria specially for her and Walter. Wilf remembers watching her as she listened to it. Her face was tipped back and tears rolled down her cheeks. Next day, in the back yard, she told me about it. 'It was beautiful,' she said. 'I hope Walter heard it.'

5

The Patient Goddess

As I sit here in Tí Neillí Mhuiris, writing about May's washing line and Kath's tears, in my mind's eye I can see a headland in Dún Chaoin. Wilf and I were there today. It stands about a hundred feet above the Atlantic, facing west to the islands and the huge expanse of sky above the waves. We parked the car by the road and walked out to the cliffs. The light was so pure we could see folds in the rocks round the island. And, half hidden in a hollow in the earth, we found what we were looking for. It was a holy well.

In Ireland, holy wells are places where springs of water

rise out of the earth. Sometimes they're marked by carvings or low walls. Sometimes they're just depressions in the ground where the water gathers in a hollow, or spills out between stones. You find them on headlands, in fields, and higher up in the mountains among barren outcrops of rock. They were seen as places where awareness of the energy of the universe was heightened and ritual gatherings of the people could support its endless flow.

St Gobnait's well in Dún Chaoin is marked by stones. Above it there's a cross cut into a flat slab. Lower down, just above the water, is a carved female head. Her blank, serene face stares out to sea. The wind has blurred her features but the carving's modern. Only a few years ago it wasn't there, and the well was just a spring rising in a rocky hollow. Today there was a bunch of wildflowers in a little bottle set low down by the water. They were still fresh. People have prayed to the saint by this well for more than a thousand years.

And for thousands of years before that, holy wells belonged to the Good Goddess, whose name here was Danú, which meant 'water'. Without water nothing can grow, so Danú was an image of the essence of life. The people who worshipped her here carved no images of her face; when they prayed by her holy wells they imagined her present in the water in the form of an immortal fish.

To the Celts Danú symbolised fertility and hope,

certainty and patience. All over the world people have shared the same idea of a powerful goddess who brings life back to their fields in springtime. She's memory and potential, the one who understands the past and holds the promise of the future. There are stories of seeds wakening to the pressure of her naked feet above them, and flowers springing up where her cloak touches the earth. All over Corca Dhuibhne people still gather at holy wells that were once sacred to the Goddess, to pray for protection and healing. Each year, my neighbours in Dún Chaoin come to the well on the headland for the 'pattern'. 'Pattern' comes from the English word 'patron', and patterns are ritual gatherings on saints' feast days. On St Gobnait's day, for as long as anyone can remember, people have gathered at the well on the cliff above the ocean to perform a ritual that has roots older than Christianity.

There are memories here of nine boatloads of people rowing from the island to Gobnait's pattern, and of crowds of people climbing from the landing place to the clifftop. Rituals associated with patterns at wells all echo each other. People circle the well, usually three, five, seven, nine or nineteen times, praying. They move in the direction of the sun. They kneel and pray. Then they bend lower to reach the water, and drink three, or seven, or nine drinks from their bare hands. Then the circling may begin again, each round marked by touching a stone or throwing a pebble in the water. Before leaving the well, something's always left behind, a flower, a feather, a pin, a rag or a coin. They're gifts to the saint to remind her of the people's prayers. Then the people go home and wait to be answered.

The parish church in Dún Chaoin is dedicated to St Gobnait. She's associated with bees, who fertilise trees and plants, and with healing. There are stories here about how she protected the people; in one she drives out invaders by turning her beehive into a bronze helmet and her bees into soldiers. In others she's one of three sisters, all powerful healers. I remember the sense of recognition I felt the first time I realised that the stories about those three sister saints, and the dates of their patterns, are all echoes of the Good Goddess. Gobnait's pattern day's 11 February, at the beginning of the Celts' season of Imbolc. Her sisters' patterns are in May, the season of Bealtaine, and at the end of July, which is the beginning of Lughnasa. Thousands of years before Christianity came to Corca Dhuibhne the people here imagined Danú as a goddess of three aspects; she was the maiden, the mother and the crone, images of the three stages of fertility. The maiden represented springtime. The mother was ripeness and harvest. And the crone was an image of withering, before the darkness of winter and the patient wait for the return of light in spring.

Today when I bent over Gobnait's well to look at the tribute of wildflowers, I saw something else had been left there. Down at the level of the water, the pointed quill of a seagull's feather was wedged between two stones. Held by the fixed quill, the feather itself reached out like a bridge. Out of the corner of my eye I saw movement in the shadow under the stones. Then a tiny shrew ran out onto the feather. She had sleek ash-coloured fur, delicate, five-clawed feet, and eyes like black pin heads in her narrow face. Her ears were like translucent pink petals. Balanced in time, her weight balanced on the quill held by the stone, she looked at me. Then the feather trembled, its shadow flickered on the water, and she ran back into the dark.

My mother often came to visit when Wilf and I had our flat in London. She got to know Kath and May as we hung washing on the line or watered the plants in the yard. And she and I would walk by the river, checking out the latest styles in the shops and people-watching in cafés. I remember her raising her eyebrows at a group of girls skimming foam off cappuccinos and licking it off their coffee spoons; she wasn't at all sure it was good manners. Then, suddenly, she picked up her own spoon one day and did it herself, announcing that 'you may as well be out of the world as out of the fashion.'

That was a quote from her own mother, my other granny, a stylish woman who'd met and married my grandfather in Dublin. He was working in the post office.

She was working in a shop. They moved back to Enniscorthy, the east-coast town Granny was born in, when my mother was eight or nine and Ireland was in the middle of a war of independence. During the war there was a curfew in Dublin but one night, after she'd been called indoors, my mother sneaked out of the house and along a hedge to play with the little girl next door. A passing patrol of the British troops that people called Black And Tans saw movement in the hedge and fired into the garden. My mother ran through the nextdoor garden without even realising she was in danger but, afterwards, poor Granny was in such a state that she insisted on leaving the city and taking her family home to Enniscorthy. They were only there a year or so when my grandfather died and Granny was left to raise her three girls with very little money. But her sister and a cousin helped, and my mother and aunts grew up with the family rule that you 'always keep the best side out'. When my mother and my aunt Kathleen left school they moved back to Dublin, to work. Evie, their sister, died young. Granny lived on in Enniscorthy till she died there in her eighties.

Although her family probably hadn't spoken Irish for generations, my Enniscorthy granny had the traditional habit of summing up life in phrases and proverbs. The Irish for 'proverbs' is *seanfhocail*, which means 'old words'. In the past, when people's speech here was peppered with them, being able to cap one with another was a valued skill. They're a distillation of inherited wisdom, sometimes wry or funny, often beautiful, and always to the point. Here in Corca Dhuibhne they're still quoted when people want to convey an idea or clinch an argument. *Níl crann sna flaithis níos airde ná crann na foighde* is one you hear often. It means 'there's no higher tree in heaven than the tree of patience.'

My Enniscorthy granny was frail by the time I remember her, but she still kept the best side out. There was a starched cloth on the polished table where we had tea when we visited; the cups were her own mother's sky blue and white china, patterned with roses; and pink biscuits with a streak of jam between mounds of sticky, coconut covered meringue were served from a cut glass biscuit barrel. For some reason, they were known as 'curly-wees'. I remember gooseberry jam, made with fruit from her garden, and 'country butter' served on thin slices of brown soda bread. The strong taste of the salty, locally made butter was almost like cheese. As a child, I wasn't sure I liked it, but it had to be eaten before moving on to a curly-wee.

There were apple trees as well as gooseberry and blackcurrant bushes in the garden. It was always said that Granny made a miraculous cough cure out of blackcurrants; I think it may just have been a spoonful of her jam dissolved in boiling water, but I remember it was warm and eased the pain.

The house in Enniscorthy was built on a hill and the long garden had a raised terrace running along one side. I remember conifers, and tall ivory-coloured lilies on thick green stems, with golden stamens and petals like curled vellum powdered with pollen. There were flagstones outside the kitchen door and a path that ran down the garden to the apple trees and fruit bushes.

One day, when I was four or five, I was sent out to play. I ran down the path at full tilt, tripped on a stone and landed flat on my front in a puddle. I can remember my nose streaming and the salty taste of tears running into my mouth as I stumbled, dripping, back up the path and into the kitchen. Granny took me into the bathroom and ran hot water from a geyser over the bath into a flowered china bowl, which fitted into a hole in a wooden washstand. Through the bathroom door I could see my mother washing my dress in the kitchen sink. After I was washed, dried, and dressed, I was given a curly-wee and told to sit on the doorstep and wait while my damp socks were hung by the fire. Granny left me there with a kiss and one of her brisk, ritual sayings. 'It's-all-over-now-throw-my-hat-in-the-sky!' I never quite knew what that meant, but my mother always said it too when things had gone wrong, and it was immeasurably comforting. Later, the three of us walked down the garden together, the mother, the child and the old woman. I remember the strength of their hands as they swung me across the puddle before we counted the knots of hard, green apples setting on the apple trees. The same trees are still there today. Spring blossom still sets as hard green apples on their gnarled branches, now propped with stakes and powdered with grey lichen.

Each autumn when I was a child, Granny would send boxes of apples on the train from Enniscorthy to Dublin, carefully tied with twine and addressed to my mother, 'to be collected'. They were cardboard cartons, provided by the local grocers, with Boland's Biscuits, Tayto Crisps, or Jaffa Oranges printed on the sides. They'd travel up in the guard's van and my brothers were sent to carry them home on the bus. If you caught the number eleven there was a walk at one end, and getting the sixty-two meant you had to walk at the other; the tarts and puddings my mother made from the apples were welcomed but the heavy boxes definitely weren't. I remember my mother teaching me to make apple tart in the kitchen in Dublin, the print of her thumb crimping the edges, and the mark of her wedding ring on the pastry scraps she'd flatten with her hand and pinch into leaves for decoration. When I look down at my hands as I type this I can see that ring on my own finger.

My mother died when Wilf and I were still living in the flat with the little concrete yard. After her death, the family house in Dublin was sold. Years earlier, when I was five, my father had taken a post as professor of history at Galway university; but the family was settled in Dublin by then, and my brothers and sisters and I were at school there. So in term time he commuted from Dublin to Galway by train, spending three nights a week in a hotel across the road from the house where he was born. By that time the barber's shop had been covered by a façade linking it to two other houses, and become a bank; and my grandfather's name, which used to be painted over the shop door, had long gone.

I don't know how my mother felt about being a single parent while he was away. But they'd decided he had to go where the work was, so no doubt she kept the best side out. On those journeys to and from Galway my father wrote books. When I write I can cut and paste and jump to any point in my own book with the click of a mouse. His clear, rigorous prose was created by hand, leaning on a board held on his knee in those swaying railway carriages. In my mind's eye I can still see his elegant, legible manuscripts, written in pencil on unused pages cut from the back of his students' exam scripts. I remember the excitement of waiting for him to arrive home on Thursday evenings, and the presents of comics and secondhand books he brought crammed into his briefcase.

After his death my mother continued to live in the Dublin house, where the walls were lined with his library of books. And after her own death, when the house was sold, the books were shared among the family. My share arrived in London in cardboard cartons tied up in twine, looking exactly like my Enniscorthy granny's boxes of apples.

Wilf had already put up as many shelves as our flat could hold, so the arrival of the books meant we had to find someplace bigger to live. When a nearby house came onto the market we jumped at it. It was a narrow, redbrick house in an Edwardian terrace and it fitted our two main criteria – there was space for the books and we could afford it. The price had a lot to do with the state it was in. Which made it an even bigger DIY project than the flat had been. But we coped, doing one room at a time and watching the boxes of books disappear under layers of plaster dust, wood shavings and paint splashes.

Living in a building site soon lost its entertainment value. I was trying to write a radio series with one hand and pull hundreds of bent carpet tacks out of the floor-boards with the other. Wilf was commissioning a series of new operas and trying to work on the house in the evenings. On one ghastly night he found dry rot in the bedroom ceiling. We'd already dealt with snails in the kitchen and bees in the roof space, but the horror of 'fruiting bodies' over our heads nearly finished me off. There were times when everything we did seemed to take twice as long as we wanted. But from the very start the joy of that house was the garden. The front door opened straight onto the street but at the back there was a jumble of overgrown shrubs, rusting dustbins and rotting lino. At first we hardly went out there. But eventually we hacked things back, propped up the sagging fence and found we had a little plot of grass surrounded on three sides by flowerbeds, a strip of concrete outside the back door, and an obsolete outside loo with a leaking roof. And, in one corner, there was a little apple tree.

At that time, everyone we knew seemed to be in the middle of a 'garden makeover'. The big thing was decking. You were supposed to recreate your boring old garden as an outside living space, seamlessly linked to your designer interior. Water features were vital. So were mirrors, lights, textures and feature walls in pink. If you had children, they needed play areas with soft-fall membrane under their bespoke, postmodern tree houses. Once you got that lot done, you decided on your 'planting'. White was considered relaxing. But you might want to go for vibrant clashing colours, to remind you of your holiday in Morocco. You got them in garden centres, laid out in sections labelled 'fragranced' or 'suitable for pots and hanging baskets'. Mostly you planted in pots. Because next year you'd be going for ornamental grasses, or channelling your inner kitchen goddess with a two-tier herb garden.

For us there wasn't time or money to embark on a makeover. Besides, by the time we got round to thinking about it, plants that had been hidden under the sagging fence and rotting lino had begun to reveal themselves.

There was a spiky hedge of japonica and forsythia mixed with flowering currants and blackthorn. There were blue-bells and roses in the flowerbeds. It was fascinating to watch them emerge. We added clumps of lily-of-the-valley, transplanted from the bed by May's back door, and a white spreading plant with many-headed flowers that came from under Kath's rose bush. When we'd left the flat she'd grubbed it out in handfuls and given it to Wilf in a paper bag, with a cheerful warning. 'You can't kill it, dear, it gets everywhere.' It did, and we grubbed out handfuls in our turn, and passed them on to anyone who'd take them. Wilf's mother gave us a new rose bush, and a little concrete frog she'd bought at B&Q. She wasn't into folklore, and the concrete frog was a world away from his origin as a totem made to express the idea of the Good Goddess who protected the land, but he came with a note that said he was 'to guard the garden'.

That year Wilf built me a long window box for an anniversary present. We filled it with herbs for summer cooking and white cyclamen that shone on the outside windowsill in winter. And beyond the little patch of lawn we had a birdbath, and a hole clipped in the hedge so we could see John.

John lived in the house behind us, with a long narrow garden that backed onto our small one. He grew runner beans and onions and broad beans, and looked after his two neat rows of pollarded apple trees. He always claimed he wasn't a gardener, he was 'a farming chap who never got back to his village after the war.' He'd joined up in 1939 and lived through one of the longest Allied campaigns, in the Far East, as a member of Britain's 'forgotten army'. He didn't talk much about the war, but he wore his greasy old army beret in the garden, and he used to tell the story of how he came home. 'We was put on a ship and come back to London, and I'd been feeling queer all the time we was at sea. I didn't know my way round London when I got here, but me mum rented this here house all through the Blitz, and I had her address on a bit of paper. And a bloke on the train told me to get on the tube till it got to the terminus and to walk along the river till I got to mum's house. So I did, but I was feeling awful queer along the way. So I knew I was due for a go of malaria. So I followed the river on till I came to where the bloke said I should, and I turned inland. And I found mum's house, and I knocked on the door. And my brother opened it. I hadn't seen him since before the war, I didn't know if he was still alive. But he was and he'd been out in the East as well. I hadn't known that. And he said, "Hello, John," he said, "you look like you're due for a go of malaria." He'd seen it before, see. So he went round the chemist and got me some quinine.'

When he recovered from his bout of malaria, John bought his mother the house she'd rented during the war.

'We'd plenty of back pay, see, because they didn't send you nothing out in the jungle.' Then, when his mother died, he lived on there alone, looking after her garden. In the evenings he'd 'drop down the Legion,' the British ex servicemen's club, for a beer. When we first spoke to him over the fence he told us our apple tree was pollinated by bees from his garden. 'I see 'em digging it out of my blossoms. Then they hops over your side and passes it on. Then you wait, see. You gotter have patience. And your apples'll come.'

I remember asking him once why he hadn't gone back to farming when his mum died. But he just shook his head. Maybe he'd settled where he was. Maybe he'd seen too much in the war. He used to get books on military history out of the library and read about the campaign he'd lived through on the ground. Once he told us that he'd never had a shot fired at him. 'My mates used to want to be beside me on patrol 'cos I never took no fire. I dunno why. I suppose my time just hadn't come.' When he told us that I thought it was wonderful. Now, looking back, I wonder if it tormented him to think that he'd lived when his companions had died.

We only ever saw John as a friendly face peering through the hole in the hedge. He'd stand on his side of the fence and whistle and, when we'd come out, he'd reach through the hedge with runner beans wrapped in newspaper, or some rhubarb 'if you fancy a pie'. Far too often we'd intend to cook them but, despite their freshness and the herbs on our windowsill, we'd end up grabbing a takeaway instead. Then the rhubarb or the beans would go off in the bottom of the fridge and we'd bin them and lie to John about how good they'd been. When I look back, I remember those gifts of wasted food that he'd patiently planted and cared for and harvested in its prime.

He died in a hospital ward where they didn't allow flowers. Sometimes we'd sneak in a sprig of rosemary or a couple of daisies in a mustard jar full of water, and he'd hide them amongst the books on his bedside locker. One day we arrived as a nurse was pulling back the curtains. As I settled our chairs by the bed, John caught Wilf's eye and sketched a thumbs-down gesture. He'd just heard from the doctor that his time had come. I think of him often now when I'm working in Neillí and Paddy's garden. I see his face in a leafy frame, like a Green Man on an English country pub sign wearing an army beret.

And now, sitting at my desk in Tí Neillí Mhuiris, I remember the first time Jack walked up the road from his farm to help Wilf plant potatoes. We'd only had Neillí's house a year then. The garden at the back was still pretty much part of the mountain: boggy, hummocky, sloping land, which we hadn't got round to thinking about. Where Con had once tended an immaculate lawn there was a waving meadow of grass and wildflowers in summer, surrounded by shaggy hedging. We thought it was pretty. Jack thought it was a waste of a good potato patch.

He walked up on a spring day, with Spot and Sailor at his heels and a spade on his shoulder. It was six weeks after Jim George had delivered the seaweed. As soon as we'd got it, following instructions, we'd spread it in a thick layer over Con's lawn. In the six weeks that had passed it had dried to a thick, black crust, burning away the grass and weeds beneath it.

Jack brought with him a length of string. Each end of the string was tied to a stick. He's not a man to waste words, so he handed one stick to Wilf and crunched across the dried seaweed to one side of the garden, paying out the string as he went. Wilf got the idea and crunched off to the opposite side. At one side of the garden, Jack hunkered down and stuck his stick in the earth. Then they both squinted down the string, with Wilf shifting position at his end, till Jack decided the line was straight. Then Wilf rammed his own stick into the ground and the three of us stood back to admire the result. The taut string, running straight as a die between the two sticks, marked the edge of our first potato ridge.

The dogs settled down in the sun. I went to make a pot of tea. Jack doesn't do tea breaks, but Wilf's English; and, besides, I wanted to check on the scones I had in the oven. When I came out again they'd dug half a ridge. Working backwards, using spades, they'd cut a straight line, through seaweed and sod, along the length of the string. Then they'd gone back to the top end, and worked backwards again along the same line, cutting and turning sods to form the start of the ridge. Jack was nearly seventy then. He moved with the minimum of effort, sliding the blade of his spade under the heavy, oblong sods and flipping them over with a turn of the handle. He had a long-handled spade, perfectly balanced for the work. Wilf, who's nearly twenty years younger, was sweating to keep up. His short-handled garden spade wasn't helping. Nor was the fact that Jack teaches by demonstration, so Wilf was having to watch like a hawk to understand what had to be done. But the real difference was that Jack was doing a job he'd learned a lifetime ago, and practised every year since. I sat on a bench by the front door, with the dogs at my feet, watching. He moved backwards in an unbroken rhythm, breathing to the swing of his spade. A robin darted out of the hedge and joined him, stabbing at the freshly turned earth for insects. Beak and blade moved steadily across the garden in counterpoint. It was like watching music.

When they finished that stage of the first ridge, they moved on to the second, using the string to keep them straight and parallel. Each ridge is three foot across.

They're separated by narrow trenches. Digging the trenches provides both the sods that form the sides of the ridges and the earth that's eventually shovelled over the seed potatoes. In Ireland, different areas and some-times even neighbouring parishes, have different ways of setting potatoes in the ridges. Jack lays sods across each ridge, like the rungs of a ladder, and plants the seed potatoes between them, in rows of three across. When each ridge is planted it's covered with earth. Then the earth's gently beaten flat with the back of a shovel. That year we had five ridges. Two and a half were set with potatoes. The others had onions, turnips, carrots and broccoli. Jack would have preferred to see cabbages; broc-coli doesn't interest him. Nor does garlic. But he likes beetroot. And he brought us up rhubarb crowns from his own garden, which we feed with manure from his cowshed.

Five ridges took more than one tea break. At some point, when Jack was having a smoke, Mike George, who was passing, came and sat on the bench beside him. Wilf had finished his tea and gone back to digging. Sailor had pushed his muzzle into Jack's hand. I was sitting on the ground, scratching Spot's ears. Mike and Jack watched the work thoughtfully, prob-ably wondering why Wilf was using that spade. They leant back against the wall, remembering Con. 'He had daffodils inside the gate.' 'He had. And he had bushes with flowers on them round the back.' 'And arbutus in the hedge there.' The paper-white daffodils still bloom in the same place; they survived several seasons under a pile of rubble we'd dumped behind the gate, and poked their green beaks out of the earth as soon as we moved it. And the arbutus was still there, half smothered by briars, though it had to wait two more years before we got round to releasing it. As I scratched Spot's ears, Mike looked at the earth Wilf was throwing over the seed potatoes. 'That's good earth,' he said, 'what did Paddy have in it?' Jack glanced at him sideways. 'Neantóga', he said, 'nettles'. Whatever else Paddy's remembered for, it isn't gardening. But when he and Neillí were living here people used to point this house out as 'the house of the seven beds', or ridges, so I suppose it was Neillí who dug and set them. I know that the seaweed that nourished her potatoes came from the same beaches where we now get ours.

If you wait till after sundown when you're earthing up potatoes, the leaves lift up just high enough for you to get the earth in under them. You do it a few weeks after you've planted them, once the stalks have reached the right height. If you try to do them sooner, or choose the wrong time of day, you can spoil the crop. If the earth is too wet or too dry you can't dig it. But if the time and weather are right, the earth falls neatly off the blade of your spade, leaving each leaf on each stalk free to draw nourishment from the sun and the rain as it grows. Then you must wait for more weeks to pass and for the stalks to flower and wither before the time comes to dig your crop.

It was here in Tí Neillí Mhuiris that I began to realise that the best things happen in their own time, not when I want them to. I'm not sure it's really sunk in yet, and Wilf's always been better at it than I am. When we first came to Corca Dhuibhne on holidays, I'd be eager to know which pub was going to have music. We'd only have a few days' break then, and I was always worried we'd miss something. Wilf was happy to take things as they came. Sometimes we'd hear that a session was planned for one pub or another. More often we'd happen on a few locals who'd bumped into each other during the day and decided to get together later on for a few tunes. They'd ramble into the pub, one after the other, choose a table, and wander over to the bar. Instrument cases would be left on the floor, and on the table. 'Aon scéal?' they'd ask, and someone would get caught up in a conversation with a friend at the bar. The kettle would be boiled to make coffee while the pints were being poured. Nothing would be hurried. Even pulling a pint of Guinness takes patience. The glass is tipped at the correct angle and slowly filled to the correct point. Then it's left to rest till it's properly settled. Then the creamy 'head' is carefully added, and it's left to rest again. Everyone knows you can't rush a good pint, any more than you can force a kettle to boil. These things take time.

Once the drinks were on the table, and people had caught up with each other's stories, they'd start to open their music cases. You never know what combination of instruments will arrive at any given session. There might be fiddles, accordions, concertinas or whistles. Sometimes there's a flute. Sometimes there's a bodhrán, the traditional skin drum. Conventionally, the music's played in unison, instead of being harmonised. Often people bring two or three instruments and swap from one to another for different tunes.

Visiting musicians are usually welcomed at sessions. But like everything else in Corca Dhuibhne, music making involves courtesy and etiquette that's easy for outsiders to miss. Everything's understated, and decisions are made with a nod or a glance, but the sequence of tunes is always led by the senior member in the group, who also calls for people to sing; 'abair amhrán!', they'll call, which means 'say a song'. There are times when someone's auntie, sitting in the corner, may shout for a particular song. Sometimes a man from the next parish stands up and recites a poem; it could be a medieval lyric he might have heard it on the radio or he might have made it up himself the day before. Sometimes a session takes on a life of its own and turns into a dance. But these things can't be demanded. They happen in their own time.

Those were the nights Wilf and I missed most when we were in London. But after years of big, classical operas written by dead composers, he wanted to work with live, contemporary composers instead. So he'd set up a company within the Royal Opera House at Covent Garden, and begun commissioning small-scale works. It was a new idea that demanded bucketfuls of time, determination and creative energy, as well as new ways to fund the work and reach out to new audiences who mightn't think opera was for them. There were lots of demands for a competition to decide which pieces were suitable for production and questions about how to establish 'what people really wanted to hear'. Wilf wasn't interested. Working with composers who'd learnt their craft from years of hard-earned experience, he wanted to prepare the ground for a new generation, set seeds, and wait to see what would grow. He stuck to his guns, the new audiences came, and the work was exhilarating. But it was also knackering, and incredibly stressful. We kept grabbing weekends in Corca Dhuibhne but, even in those days before emails on iPads, there'd be calls about work as soon as we'd pulled up in the hire car at our B&B. It got harder and harder to find weekends we could both take off together. In those years we arrived here and crashed; and resented the fact that soon our snatched breaks would be over. We never found the well on the headland in Dún Chaoin. And, though we'd driven past this house we'd one day live in, we'd no idea that across the road another holy well had been springing from the earth for thousands of years.

Three years after we bought Tí Neillí Mhuiris, Jack's nephew, Terry, arrived one day with his girlfriend, Cliodhna. For months I'd been wanting Wilf to choose an instrument and start playing the music he enjoyed so much in the pubs. But whenever I'd suggest buying a whistle, or having a go at a fiddle, he'd tell me he wanted to wait. It wasn't the right time yet. Something would come along. Then Terry and Cliodhna came, and they brought a concertina. Cliodhna's father, who's a stonemason, had been given it when he was working on a house. He'd given it to her in his turn, but she hadn't been that interested. Then Jack, who misses nothing, had heard of it and remembered that Wilf liked the music sessions.

If you're used to playing classical piano you have to rewire your brain to play a concertina. The left and right hands work together differently and there are several ways of getting the same note, depending on what button you hit and whether you push or pull. Traditionally, music here is learnt by ear, not from notes on a page. And even if it is written down, people here don't use the classical form of notation. I've written all that as if I know what I'm talking about but, actually, I don't. The traditional music stuff's a whole other book to be written, that's Wilf's, not mine. All I know is that when Cliodhna handed him the concertina he took it in his hand and knew it was his instrument. When she left she told him to keep it as long as he wanted to. He did, until we bought one of his own.

Now, years later, he's playing in sessions down in the village. But I think my favourite times are when he's playing on the bench here outside Tí Neillí Mhuiris, when the garden's full of life and nourishment and there's a sense that, even though there's work to be done, there's time for music and stories as well.

Last night I was reading a book by Robin Flower. He's the young Englishman with bare feet and no hat in the photo of the meitheal of men who built the Blasket island slipway. That photo was taken a hundred years ago, when Flower came to the island to study Irish. He stands with his head thrown back and a huge smile on his face as he looks at the camera. The island men look a bit self conscious and there's an overseer with a watch chain across his waistcoat and a natty white sunhat, looking pompous. But Robin Flower's just having a wonderful time. It was his first trip to the island and after it he couldn't keep away. I remember reading his books about it when I was a student. Lots of the books I read at university were dry and dense, and I waded through them the same way I'd struggled with Peig's book at school. But everything Flower wrote is touched by the same energy and delight that beams out of his photo on the slipway.

Once, when he was out walking on the island, he met an old man digging potatoes in a field. 'You have an unsociable way with you,' said the man, 'don't you give people a greeting when you pass them on the road?' 'Yes,' said Flower, 'But I didn't see you over the wall.' 'A man should have eyes in every corner,' said the man. And he laid his spade crossways over the furrow where he'd been digging. Then he sat down on it, and invited Flower to sit on the other end. They sat there together in the field. Then the man began to speak a poem. After a little while, the poem became a story about the feats of the warrior hero, Fionn Mac Cumhaill. It was full of long, crafted sentences, strange words and repeated sound patterns. In his book, Flower says that when the story was finished, the old man caught his eye. 'I have kept you from your dinner,' he said. It was a ritual courtesy that belongs to an ancient tradition of storytelling. Flower answered it with another. He said 'a tale is better than food.' I said that to a neighbour here once and he shook his head.

'I don't know if it is,' he said, 'but I'd say that both would nourish you.'

This morning, when we came back from Gobnait's well at Dún Chaoin, we walked over to the well in the field across the road from Tí Neillí Mhuiris. The saint that people used to pray to here was called Mo-Laga. I read that in a book when we first came here. But we had to live here, and wait a while, before we heard the older story that belongs to that low spring of water, still rising between scattered stones. We heard it when we walked down to Jack's farm one evening, to watch the news on his television. We watched stories about war and recession and bankers' bonuses. Then there was the weather forecast. I'd put a pocketful of sweets on the table and later, as we ate them, I asked Jack about Mo-Laga's well. And he told us this story. 'One time in the village they wanted water to boil the potatoes. And they went to the well in that field and drew water and they put it in a pot on the fire. But the water wouldn't boil at all. And they waited and it was no good to them, and they looked inside in the pot. And there was a small fish inside in the pot with the potatoes, and the water wouldn't boil with him. So they took him out of the pot and they carried him back and put him in the well. And the potatoes boiled after that.'

People prayed to St Mo-Laga at the well across our road long before potatoes were ever grown here. And the story of water refusing to boil because it's been taken from a holy well is older still, older than the time of the people of the goddess Danú. All across the world, from India to this last inhabited place in mainland Europe, the same story's been passed from mouth to ear for countless millennia. And, wherever it's told, it never loses its central image of the Good Goddess as a fish. I heard it after the six o'clock news, sitting in Jack's kitchen. Sailor was dead then, and Spot had two brindled pups playing beside her on the floor.

The day I fell down in my granny's garden in Enniscorthy, I was left sitting on the step till my socks dried. It was a high, square slab of stone outside the kitchen door, shaped by a mason's chisel. Generations of feet had crossed it as they went down the garden, to hang out washing, pick fruit, gather flowers, and rescue children from puddles. Over the years each foot that trod on the stone had made a slightly deeper hollow in its centre. So one day, Granny, who liked to keep the best side out, decided to have it lifted and turned over. That would bury the old, worn bit, create a new, flat surface and cost less than buying a new step. So a man was offered a fair price to dig down, get a spade under the stone, lift it and turn it over. Granny was in the kitchen when she heard him outside, laughing. When he'd turned the step over it was thick with earth. So he'd chucked a bucket of water on it. And there on the underside was another hollow, made by other passing feet. Long before Granny's time, someone else had turned the stone step over, wanting to keep the best side out.

As I write this I see three figures moving in memory: maiden, mother and crone. I can feel strong hands holding mine under the apple trees in Enniscorthy, where countless feet passed from kitchen to garden and back again, wearing hollows in the stone. Then light trembles on water, and John's finger touches a sprig of rosemary in a mustard jar, hidden in a pile of books. And in my mind's eye I see patient women circling an ancient spring of water on the headland, still hoping for healing, peace and strength.

6

The Way into the West

'**B**rendan came down from Mount Brandon and he and his companions set out for the Isle of the Blessed. They put out from Brandon Creek and they sailed into the west till they came to an island where there was a dog. And then there was another island, where sheep were grazing alone. And there was an island where nothing grew, and they landed on it and they lit a fire. But the island wasn't an island at all. It was a fish as big as an island. And the fish dived down into the sea. And then they sailed on over waves that were rutted like a frosty field, past a silver pillar wrapped in net and past rocks that were pillars of fire. They sailed for seven years. And some of them left, I think, and some were killed. And there was a man who lived alone on an island and was fed by an otter. But in the end, because they kept on and had courage, they found the Isle of the Blessed.'

I heard that story when I was here as a student, badgering everyone I met to see if they had versions of the texts I'd read at university. The man who told it to me ended with a proverb, *is glas iad na cnoic i bhfad uainn*. It means 'far away hills are green'. The people who live here know all about the longing to sail beyond the western horizon. And the longing, when you get there, to come home.

Brandon Creek's six miles or so from Tí Neillí Mhuiris. Brendan was a fifth-century Irish saint and both the creek and the mountain are named after him, though the spelling is different. The story of his voyage was a hit all over medieval Europe. It was written down about four hundred years after his death but people were sitting round fires telling it long before that. And long before Brendan's time there were the other voyagers, in older stories, who set to sea in glass boats to find islands where happiness lasts forever and a hundred years pass like a single day. Those were the pagan voyagers who met Manannán Mac Lir, the sea god who sang between the glory of the ocean and the high arc of the sky. Brendan and his monks met birds who sang different songs in praise of a different, Christian, god. But each story mirrors the other, and the same human fears and longings echo in both. Longing for something new and better and exciting. Fear of the unknown.

It was Wilf's Aunt Alice from Arizona who brought us to the next turn in the long road that led us here to Tí Neillí Mhuiris. Alice is a tall woman with great legs and a great fashion sense. She probably inherited the legs from her mum, who adored shoes and insisted on squeezing into killer heels till the day she died. Alice and her brother Eric, who was Wilf's dad, were born in Tottenham, in North London. Their father was a clerk in the Gas Board. Later the family moved to Hoddesdon, just outside London. But old roots strike deep; Wilf and his brother still support Tottenham Hotspurs because their dad was born beside the football ground. Apparently it's not the most enviable inheritance, but it seems that in these things you don't get a choice. Eric was in the Air Force during the Second World War. There are photos of him in Egypt, in a cravat and an impressive moustache, and one of him and Alice with their arms round each other's shoulders outside their Hoddesdon home. Alice is wearing killer heels.

While Eric was in Egypt Alice went into the Land Army. I imagine she never climbed onto her tractor without first touching up her lipstick. Land Girls worked long hours in the fields doing the work of farm workers who'd joined the fighting services. Some must have staggered back to their billets each night and collapsed into bed. But Alice and her mates went dancing. Then, at some point when she was out jitterbugging, she met an American GI and agreed to marry him after the war. When the time came, her mum and dad didn't want her to go. Eric had been demobbed and the family was together again for the first time in years. But Alice was in love. And, according to herself, she was 'a very determined girl'. She had to wait two years before she got a berth on a decommissioned troopship taking GI brides and fiancées to America. There were queues and medical examinations and regulations about how much money each girl could take out of the country. There was continued concern from her parents. But she packed her bags and set out for her new life.

I talked to Alice on the phone last night. She's still in America, living in a retirement community in Arizona and lovingly cared for by her American family. When she picked up the phone she sounded old and a little tired. But she remembers that voyage as if it was yesterday, and the more we talked about it, the more energetic she became. By the end of the conversation she was roaring with laughter. 'It was so horrible! There were twenty of us to a cabin and every one of us was sick. They'd given us these terrible vaccinations, I don't know what they were for. But they made us so sick! And then the food was awful. And we were throwing up. Oh, my! It was so bad. And it was supposed to be so romantic!' By the second day they were feeling better. Some of them even managed to struggle up on deck. 'There was all this ocean. Just grey waves for miles and miles. And we were all saying "my! we're a long way from home!" And we kept on travelling over those grey waves. And then we sailed in past the Statue of Liberty. We were young and we'd made it. We were there!'

But as soon as she got there things went wrong. The GI turned out to have a girl at home, and Alice found herself alone in a strange country, with hardly a penny and nowhere to stay. It must have been terrifying. But even if she could have found her fare home, she was damned if she was going to go back and admit what had happened. So, being Alice, she put on her best dress, walked into the nearest big store, announced she was a fashion model from London, and got herself a job as a mannequin. 'Up and down the floor, hon, for hours. The walking nearly killed me. And the money hardly kept me in nylons.' Twenty years later she'd become head buyer at one of the biggest fashion companies in America. And along the way she'd met the real love of her life, a guy called Ray, who became her husband. Like thousands of other girls who'd made the trip before her, she'd survived and made herself a new life.

If you walk up the Clasach from Dún Chaoin today there's a place where you can turn and look back for a last glimpse of the islands. People call it The Place of Goodbyes. In the past, some of the saddest gatherings in Ireland were called American Wakes. Traditionally when someone died here, the body was laid out in the house, where neighbours would gather to pass the night with the family till the coffin was buried next day. These gatherings, to support the family and pray for the dead, were called wakes. They're still held in Corca Dhuibhne, though now the neighbours tend to visit the house in the evening, rather than staying there all night. Neillí Mhuiris's mother, Bríghid, was waked in the house where I'm writing this. The neighbours who came here would have sat by the fire here till morning, telling stories, saying prayers and 'keening', or crying, for the dead. If the person who died was old, and the death had been easy and natural, the grief was often broken by periods of storytelling and dancing; there'd be reminiscences about the past and even arrangement for marriages in the future. Death was just part of life. At wakes, coffins were supported on two chairs, which were ritually knocked over as the coffin was lifted and carried out through the door. At the graveside there was keening as it was lowered into the earth. But at American Wakes there were no coffins. They were gatherings held the night before young emigrants left home. In those days, before telecommunications and cheap travel, their families never expected to hear their voices, or see their faces, again.

It was the young and the strong who left, looking for a new life and a chance to send money home to the old people. They'd spend the night before their journey talking, singing and dancing for the last time with their families and friends. The old women would sit by the fire praying and keening. Tobacco, snuff and whiskey would be shared, as they were at wakes for the dead. In the grey light before dawn, the emigrants would eat their last meal by the family hearth. On the island they'd walk down the cliff path to the slipway and launch their traditional fishing boats; they're called *naomhóga*, canoe shaped vessels, with no keels, made of tar and canvas stretched on a timber frame. Then, raising the sails and using slender, wooden oars, crews of men would take the light handmade craft across the Blasket Sound. There are stories of the old women standing on the clifftop, waving their black shawls and keening as each naomhóg crossed the water to Dún Chaoin.

Every village here lost people to emigration. The older people can remember aunts and uncles setting out for America alone, aged fourteen or fifteen. Some had hardly a word of English. Some had never been farther from home than Dingle town. Carrying bags and bundles, with their tickets or the money for their passage carefully hidden in their clothes, the boys and girls from Dún

Chaoin and the island would climb the Clasach. At The Place of Goodbyes, they'd stop for a last word to their families and neighbours, and their last look at the island. Then they'd turn their backs to the life they'd known, and their faces to another world. On foot, or by train, they'd make their way to the coastal ports and travel on by ocean liner. Sometimes they left the ships in England, in some cases cheated by officials who told them they'd reached America. Other Irish emigrants travelled on across the Atlantic, to Boston, Chicago and New York or, farther still, to Canada. But mostly, if they came from the island and the villages back west, their journey's end was Springfield, Massachusetts.

When there were no films or television to show them what to expect, the contrast between their home and the places these teenagers came to must have been unimaginable. Some didn't survive the uprooting. But many found new lives. Many of their descendants in America today speak Irish, quote the same proverbs, tell the same stories, and play the same music that's still heard here in Corca Dhuibhne. And every year emigrants come back across the ocean to visit the place they still call home.

I don't know if Alice thought she'd go back to her home in Hoddesdon. She probably imagined bringing home her soldier husband and introducing him to her family. Instead, like other emigrants before her, she hid the fact that things hadn't gone as she'd hoped. In fact she never told her family what had happened, and Wilf grew up with the story that Alice's GI died in an air crash as he was flying home from his posting in Germany to marry her. Actually Alice had gritted her teeth and built her new life alone, and eventually met Ray in the fashion industry. It was years later, when her own parents, her brother Eric, and even Ray himself were dead, that she told Wilf and me the truth. I remember his jaw dropping in astonishment and the ice clinking in Alice's gin and tonic as she laughed. 'What, you think I was going to admit I'd been dumped? I'd never have lived it down! Anyway, it would have worried them.' She shrugged and lit a cigarette. 'What the heck, he did me a favour. I did pretty good in the end.'

She did better than good. Ray and Alice were brilliant together. They were best friends and work colleagues for years before they married. Afterwards they set up their own business. Then years later, Ray was diagnosed with cancer, so because they both loved sailing, they decided to sell up and spend their last few months together travelling on their boat. A year after that Ray was still going strong and they'd had enough of sailing. So they docked the boat and opened a shop. It was years later still, with Ray and the shop both doing well, that they decided to take a break and come to Ireland.

That was when Wilf and I were still working on our new house in London. I was writing for television and radio. Wilf was commissioning operas. I'd started teaching microphone technique at drama schools and script analysis to film students as well. He'd got into running a summer school for contemporary composers. We'd also both developed bad backs. One day, rushing to a rehearsal, he'd suddenly found himself flat on the floor at Waterloo station, in hideous pain and unable to move. He opened his eyes to ask for help and saw a sea of moving legs, parting on either side of him and sweeping past without stopping. Everyone's head was turned to look the other way. Eventually, he managed to crawl into a shop on his elbows and knees, and get to a phone. People had stepped aside as he pulled himself across the station precinct.

After that we told ourselves we needed to slow down a bit. But I'm not sure we did. Besides, we felt we could always recharge our batteries in Corca Dhuibhne. By then our families had joined us there for occasional weekends and we'd all stayed at John and Mary Curran's guesthouse in Dingle. It's a modern house, built on a plot above the town, with glorious views over Dingle Harbour. We'd fly over, hire a car, and drive late into the night, falling into bed when we got there and waking in the morning to eat breakfast in the sunny conservatory. Then we'd walk and drive, hang out in the pubs, or just sit by the fire, reading.

One night, in Dick Mack's pub, we came up with the idea of a family gathering at the bar there on the ninth of the ninth nineteen-ninety. Anyone who was free was to be there at nine pm, and no one would know who was coming till they arrived. Wilf and I weren't the only ones with crowded lives, so we set off from London that September prepared for no one but ourselves to turn up in Dick Mack's. We weren't bothered. It was a daft arrangement anyway, and we were happy just to be going back to Dingle.

We got there on September the eighth and drove our hire car over the mountain, wondering who might turn up the next day. The following night, at eight forty-five precisely, we were sitting in Dick Mack's. It's a small, dark brown pub, warm, friendly and crowded. There's always a roar of chat or the sound of singing. I remember it from my first visits to Mrs Hurley's. If you were staying back west when I was a student it wasn't easy to get lifts into Dingle. And, anyway, the university frowned on it. You were here to speak Irish, not English, and the place to do that was back west, where everyone spoke it. Not in town, where some people didn't. But sometimes a group of students would hitch a lift or catch a bus and spend the day hanging out in Dingle and drinking pints in Dick Mack's. Then we'd walk out and sit on the bridge at the edge of the town, hoping to be picked up by someone we knew who'd be driving home back west.

In those days, Dick Mack's smelt of porter, tobacco smoke and leather. It was the place to go if you needed a strap mended, or to buy a piece of leather for a patch. At a counter on one side you could buy boots and shoes, and have them soled and heeled. On the other side you could sit at a long bar drinking creamy pints of porter. There was a 'snug', or little booth, inside the door, with a hatch through to the bar. Women could drink there without comment; or deals could be done in private without half the town looking on and giving advice. On the shop side there were shelves crammed with shoe-boxes, cobbler's tools and parcelled-up boots for collection. On the bar side there were shelves of bottles and glasses, tins of tobacco, boxes of cigarettes and matches, and a large clock on the wall. Built into the shelving were glass-fronted cupboards. Behind the shining beer pumps were jars of cloves and of sugar, and slices of lemon, for making hot ports and hot whiskies.

On the night of the ninth of the ninth nineteen ninety, Wilf and I sat there with one eye on the clock and the other on the door, telling ourselves no one was coming. Then, on the dot of nine, the door opened and in walked Alice and Ray. They were the only people to turn up for the gathering – all the way from America.

Ray had Irish roots. I don't know what part of the country his people came from, and I don't think he cared. None of his family had ever made the long journey back across the Atlantic. So for him, just being in Ireland was enough. They'd flown in to Shannon Airport and picked up a hire car. So they were tired when they arrived. Ray was unused to the narrow, twisting roads and driving on the left. Like me, the first time Wilf and I came here together, Alice had held her breath for most of their climb over the Conor pass. 'But then, oh my gosh, we looked down at Dingle and the ocean, and the colours, and those green fields with the little stone walls . . .' She was sitting on a bar stool with her elegant legs crossed at the ankles and a gin and tonic in her hand. She grinned at Ray, who was downing a pint. 'Believe me, now we've finally made it, I'm determined to have a good time.'

The big thing for Alice and Ray here was the boats. Ray couldn't believe the tar-and-canvas naomhóga. 'They really put out to sea in those things?' He was still impressed even when he found that some are now made of fibreglass. I've seen eager tourists get the polite brush-off from boatmen here who wanted to get on with their work. But Ray's questions must have shown he knew what he was talking about. Anyway, he came back to Currans with more information about the Dingle fishing fleet than I'd managed to pick up in twenty years.

At the guesthouse John produced ice and cut glass tumblers so Alice and Ray could relax with a drink in their room in the evenings. Wilf and I would join them to make plans for the next day. We hadn't done tourist things in Corca Dhuibhne for ages, but Ray and Alice were up for everything.

So we drove down long, winding roads and walked long, empty beaches. There was hogweed on the ditches and long tendrils of curling briar. The fuchsia was scarlet and purple and the last of the summer montbretia was still orange and bright neon-green. We had new-laid eggs and soda bread for breakfast at Currans, and drank strong tea by turf fires in the small pubs back west. One day we crossed the Clasach and ate crab sandwiches and black porter cake outside the pottery café in Dún Chaoin. And Wilf took over the driving when the mountain roads got so narrow that the briars whipped the sides of the car and Alice covered her eyes.

Each evening, sitting in their room, they'd produce sheaves of leaflets and we'd plan the next day's adventures. Ray was fascinated by the idea that the people of Danú carved spirals and circles on single standing stones. When Wilf and I came here on our honeymoon, I'd dragged him up muddy lanes and into high fields, looking for them. But, after several evenings spent washing socks and scraping our boots in B&Bs, he'd refused to wade through another bog until we bought wellies. Next day, we'd found a shop in Dingle that sold wheelbarrows, builders' supplies, chicken feed and galvanised iron gates. Hanging up behind the counter were bundles of large green wellies, tied together with twine. Later on, protected by stout rubber and thick knitted socks, we drove back west again and strode up mountains. I don't remember having wellies when Ray and Alice were here. So Alice probably strode up mountains in killer heels. But we found carved stones in high fields, marked with the spiral symbol of life's endlessly turning wheel. I remember Alice tracing it with her finger and smiling up at Ray.

That night, back at Currans, Ray was still fired up by archaeology. 'How about this place called Dún Beg? It says here it's a promontory fort, what's that?' I was about to launch into a lecture on Iron Age settlements when Alice looked up from a leaflet. 'OK, enough archaeology! I have got to meet this guy Fungi.' And she held up a picture of a bottle-nosed dolphin.

Nearly thirty years ago, Paddy Ferriter, the Dingle Harbour lighthouse keeper, noticed a wild dolphin had decided to follow the fishing fleet to and from the port. Back since the time of voyagers like St Brendan, there've been stories here about sea creatures making contact with people out in boats. Bottlenosed dolphins aren't usually found singly, though, so the fishermen didn't expect this one to hang about long. But each time they put to sea he appeared again and followed them. Two years later they'd named him Fungi and he'd started to entertain them by racing with their boats. No one knows how or why Fungi lost touch with the dolphins he must have swum with since he was born. But since 1984 he's been a big tourist attraction in Dingle. All through the summer, boatloads of visitors are taken out from the port with the promise of their money back if they don't catch a glimpse of the dolphin. He's never failed to turn up.

The day after Alice found his picture in the leaflet, the four of us walked to the pier and joined a boatload of dolphin fans. Over the years Fungi and the boatmen have worked up an act. A boat sets out, full of excited kids, and adults carrying cameras. At first there's no sign of the dolphin and everyone scans the waves, hoping their trip won't have been wasted. It seems like the boat's going to give up and turn round, when, suddenly, there's a flash of grey in the water, cameras click, and everyone starts shouting and pointing. For a while you only see the shining back streaking through the waves. Then Fungi really goes into his act. When he first came to Dingle he was timid and inquisitive, eager to follow the boats but unsure how to relate to them. Now he's a master of timing. His favourite trick is to appear at one side of the boat, leaping through the waves, which brings everyone to the rail in hopes of touching or filming him. Then he disappears and people groan and relax, and start sending photos from their phones to their mates back in the office. Then, with a huge splash, he'll suddenly leap vertically out of the water on the other side of the boat, twisting in the air and hurling spray over the screaming, shouting passengers. Sometimes he'll leap straight over the boat, showering his fans with shining drops of water before he nose dives into the sea and skims away. It's almost impossible not to believe he's laughing. Alice and Ray, Wilf and I shouted with the rest, and crowded from one side of our boat to the other. Then, as the boatman made a wide curve and set course for port again, Fungi's shining grey back loped through the water beside us, escorting us back to land.

Fungi doesn't just play with the tourist boats. He still follows the fishermen, and he joins swimmers, divers and canoeists. He loves windsurfers, skimming along beside them and bobbing up to capsize them. He's even delighted by kids paddling on the beach. And, instinctively, he seems to sense illness and frailty. He's gentle and calm around ill and handicapped swimmers, gliding serenely beside them as if he's aware of their state. There's a theory, called biophilia, that suggests human beings have an instinctive bond with other living systems, and that exploring it can benefit your health. That day, as the boat skimmed back across Dingle Harbour, I eavesdropped on one of the other passengers describing a randomised, controlled trial done by researchers at Leicester General Hospital, in England; the published results had concluded that a holistic drug-free approach which included interaction with wild dolphins had a significant positive effect on patients with mild to moderate depression. That night, over dinner, I mentioned it to Ray. He grinned and said it didn't surprise him. Some people say Fungi's not wild;

that he can't be, given his willingness to leave the ocean and hang out with human beings. But nobody's trained him or offered him bribes. He catches his own fish at the harbour mouth. No one knows exactly where he goes in winter, though the fishermen say he probably has to travel quite far to find food. But each year, at the same time, he's here again in his adopted home.

The year that Wilf and I found Tí Neillí Mhuiris we visited our old neighbour, May, in London. She'd moved into a local care home, where she had her own room, someone to do her big wash every week, and a garden to sit in. There was a labrador dog, whose job was to take the residents for little walks. Like Fungi, he seemed to understand frailty. When kids came visiting their grannies he'd gallop round chasing balls and rolling on the grass, but when he was on duty he'd pad gently round the grounds, suiting his pace to a wheelchair or the elderly ladies with walking sticks.

One day when we arrived, May was bubbling with suppressed laughter. 'Guess who's turned up.' We couldn't guess. 'Rose,' she said. We thought she'd got a bit confused. We knew Rose had gone to Sri Lanka. I wondered if, in old age, May was being revisited by memories of her neighbour from hell. She read my face and shook her head. 'No, she's here. They've given her room twelve. She said she didn't like it in Sri Lanka, so she came back. All that way! I told her when she left, I said "you're a fool to yourself, you won't like it when you get there and you won't get your flat back if you come home." But Rose don't listen. Never did. The other man's grass was always greener. That was her problem. And now she's turned up like a bad penny to bully us all to death!'

Actually, I think the return of her old sparring partner gave May a new lease of life. She lived till her daughter, Margaret, managed to make the long journey from Australia to see her. Then she died quietly in her sleep. Years before, May had told me that her husband, Jim, had been raised in an orphanage and joined the Merchant Navy in his teens. 'He'd no roots of his own, love, so he took to the sea.' When she died we found she'd left us a letter saying she wanted her ashes scattered under the same bush as Jim's at the local crematorium. We went there one damp day and followed an official as he checked the records and led us across the grass to the right spot. When he'd tipped the little box of ashes over the earth we walked back to the road and found an underpass leading to a supermarket. Then we toasted May and Jim in plastic cups of tea, sitting at yellow plastic tables in the coffee shop. That autumn Wilf brought tubers of May's lily-of-the-valley here to Neillí Mhuiris's garden. We'd uprooted it once before, when we'd taken some from the bed outside May's back door to the garden of our London house. It had survived that first move, and flourished under the spiky shrubs in the hedge. But it didn't survive the second uprooting.

Years after her visit here with Ray, Alice came back to Corca Dhuibhne. Wilf and I were still coming regularly to Dingle town to stay at Currans. Wilf had left Covent Garden by then and we'd finished the DIY on the London house. I'd begun sitting on committees, chairing board meetings and going to conferences on behalf of two writers' organisations. We'd set up a company together, working in music, theatre and television. Then, on a trip to New York, we'd borrowed a loft apartment in Tribeca and found its open-plan layout made wonderful work-spaces. So when we got home we'd designed and built a mini version in our London attic. It made a high, open space with unexpected angles, empty except for a couple of chairs and a steel desk with a glass top so thick that its edge shone turquoise when the sun hit it. The desk was a one-off, manufactured for a 1930s designer; I'd found it going for a song in the For Sale ads in our local newspaper. Towards the end of that building work, Wilf was removed to A&E after a thoughtless moment with a Stanley knife. He began his next rehearsal period wearing a black leather fingerstall, which brought an unlikely edge of menace to his mild, unobtrusive style of directing.

Our work schedule then was relentless. We got into multimedia and discovered that studying folktales had

made me better at lateral links and non-linear information provision than most of the techno-geeks we worked
with. We won awards for innovation. For a nanosecond
we were big in Japan. For another, entirely unrelated,
nanosecond I wrote for *Cosmopolitan*. We had shows in
Sydney, Australia, and Wilf worked with his brother
James in Florida. Separately and together, we collabo-
rated with talented poets, playwrights, producers, direc-
tors and composers, which was brilliant. But, basically,
it was just the two of us, working against deadlines and
worrying about finding the next job. In those crowded
years, whenever we spoke to Alice on the phone she was
sympathetic. She knew all the problems of cash flow
and uncertainty that go with working freelance. Then
one day we got a call from her. Ray had died and she
wanted to revisit Ireland. 'We were so happy there, and
I really need a rest.' But she couldn't bear to stay at
Currans, which had felt like her home from home with
Ray.

A rest sounded like a good idea. I rang Mary Curran,
who immediately understood. She sent her condolences
to Alice and gave me the numbers of places to stay that
she was happy to recommend. Then she mentioned a
woman called Síle Gorman, who lived back west. 'She's
taken guests for years, but she's just rebuilt her place and
it's beautiful. I don't know if she's open for business yet.
But you could give her a ring.' So I rang Síle. Her voice

on the phone was pleasant, though for a moment I thought she sounded doubtful. Later she told me she hadn't quite been ready to open on the dates we'd wanted, but that when she heard Alice's story she decided to take us anyway. We made the arrangements on the phone. It wasn't till I'd put it down, and told Wilf, that I took in the fact that we were going back west.

So on a summer evening, Alice, Wilf and I drove over the mountain, up the steep streets of Dingle town, and out along the last eight miles of the tapering peninsula. When we got to Gorman's the sky was a blaze of scarlet and gold, and a path of light was shimmering across the ocean towards the setting sun. Síle met us with smiles and open hands. Then, while Vincent cooked our dinner, Alice, Wilf and I took drinks out to a table in the garden. We sat there, facing the horizon, as the sun disappeared into the ocean and the huge sky turned silver and pink, like mother of pearl. The sharp edges of the cliffs that curved round the harbour darkened and softened. In the flowerbeds beside us, the lilies glowed in the dusk. I remembered something a Blasket islander had said about the fishermen he'd known and worked with who had died. He'd looked out to the west, where the sun dipped into the ocean. 'Is dócha go bhfuil said ina mbeathaig fós ag iascach ansan, agus ná cíonn tú iad,' he said. 'I suppose they're still alive fishing out there, and you don't see them.'

Years later, after we'd bought Tí Neillí Mhuiris, Alice made a final visit here to Corca Dhuibhne. She was older and a little bit bent, still elegantly dressed but wearing walking shoes. She laughed when I mentioned them. 'I've been here before, honey, I know what it takes!' That evening we walked down the road to introduce her to Jack and she insisted on being photographed beside his tractor. It reminded her of the one she'd driven during the war. When we got back to the house Wilf offered her a gin and tonic. 'Oh, I think so,' she said. 'It's my time of the evening.' When Ray died she'd changed the times of all their shared daily rituals, consciously reshaping her old life and coming to terms with her new one.

We sat by Neillí's fire talking about holidays and photographs, and Alice remembered the time her mum and dad had come to visit her in America. There's a black and white photo, taken on that visit, of Alice and her mum posing beside a sleek, 1950s convertible. Alice, with a fringe, a tiny waist and a circular skirt, looks like one of the Pink Ladies in *Grease*. Her mum, leaning against the car's bonnet, has a new handbag bought for the holiday, and a pair of killer heels. There are photos like it in albums all over Corca Dhuibhne, taken on trips to emigrant relatives in Springfield, and Boston and Chicago, and New York. When I mentioned that photo to Alice she nodded, remembering her parents' visit. 'I think my mother was glad to see for herself that I was OK.' I asked if she hadn't been tempted to tell her what really happened when she'd arrived to marry her GI. 'Oh no, honey, never. I never could. Anyway, it didn't matter by then.' So that was a story left untold.

Later in the evening Alice talked about Ray. 'He really was my best friend as well as my husband. You can't replace that. But you have to go on.' Wilf threw more turf on the fire and we chatted on, about the trip we'd all taken to see Fungi, and the time Alice and Ray had sold up their business and spent what they'd thought were his last months together on their boat. Alice laughed, remembering how they'd got bored and gone back to work, and Ray kept on living. 'I'll tell you one thing, and you better remember it – you never know what's going to happen to you, so you might as well enjoy every minute.' She squared her shoulders and knocked back her gin and tonic. And there was the very determined girl from Hoddesdon again, sailing uncharted waters on her own.

People here in Corca Dhuibhne have always said St Brendan's story's a description of a real voyage by Irish monks, who sailed north west across the Atlantic in a naomhóg till they landed in North America. If it is, they got there about three hundred years before the Viking explorer Leif Ericson, and a thousand years before

Christopher Columbus. In Brendan's story, the silver pillar wrapped in a net, and the rocks that were pillars of fire may be images of icebergs and volcanoes. The sea that was rutted like a frosty field suggests ice floes, which aren't found in the ocean around Ireland, but are found farther north, towards Iceland. So in 1976 a British explorer called Tim Severin decided to set up a practical experiment to see if Brendan's voyage could have been done. He stitched together forty-nine ox hides, stretched them over a wooden frame, and created a sea-going naomhóg, which he called the *Brendan*. Then he put together a crew, and set sail from Brandon Creek in Maytime. By June, the *Brendan* had reached the Faroe Isles which, according to legend, was where Brendan and his monks found the grazing sheep. By July, they'd reached Iceland. Less than two months later, they landed in Newfoundland. Severin's a completely practical man. He says that he still doesn't know if the first ship to reach the New World set sail from Brandon Creek. What he does know is that it could have done.

That story of Brendan's voyage belongs to a class of Irish stories called *immrama*. In each one a group of companions sets out to find an Otherworld beyond the western horizon. I can remember the excitement here when Tim Severin proved that Brendan could have made it to the New World. I suppose the links between this community and the emigrant communities in Springfield and Boston are so strong that it's fascinating to think that people could have been travelling from Corca Dhuibhne to America for millennia. But there's another theory about immrama. It's said that they're images of spiritual journeys, expressions of ancient voyages into the human mind, looking for truth. They start with visions and longings. The voyagers are drawn towards the sunset, seeking light. They meet mystical animals and monstrous fish. They cross oceans rutted like frosty fields and pass rocks like pillars of fire. But they travel on with courage. And all the time they're searching for insights into the shared soul of the universe; the links between life forms; and their own deepest frailties and fears.

7

Building an Ark

L ast night I was woken by the sound of the wind. A gale had begun to blow from the north. Suddenly the weather's turned cold and the potatoes Wilf and Jack earthed up a couple of weeks ago are suffering; since last night the north wind's been driving straight along the ridges, tattering the stalks. As I lay there, warm under the duvet, I could feel each gust that whirled down the mountain and crashed against the gable end, like waves battering a boat's hull. The walls here in Tí Neillí Mhuiris are two foot thick and on the outside they're faced with mortar. But at night, in an unrelenting storm, the house seems to leap and shudder in response to the driving wind.

It's a good roof now, so I wasn't frightened, like Paddy, that the wind would lift it. Rooted in the earth, the house enclosed and protected me. But I couldn't sleep. So, as the doors rattled and sticks and soaking leaves were driven against the windowpanes, I found myself remembering the chapter I'd just written, and you've just read, and the story of Brendan's boat. In that story, and in the older immrama it echoes, the boats of hide and timber, crystal and glass, are images of the arks, or containers, people all over the world have made through the ages, to preserve what they value and have learnt.

When I was small my father worked in the national museum in Dublin. I remember playing on the floor of his room there, and being taken by the porters to see things they thought would entertain me, like the antique dolls. But the dolls in their glass cases frightened me; I knew their bodies were stuffed with horsehair and I didn't like the sense of arrested decay in the rust-mould on their skirts. For me, the best things in the museum belonged to the Iron Age Celts. There were ring-beads of translucent black glass with yellow inlays spiralling round them. There were twisted gold collars with gorgeous fluted ends, and necklaces plaited from gold wire. There were amber beads and inlaid boxes, and a war-trumpet with sinuous tendrils round its slender tube and flowers round its mouth. Best of all, there was a little gold boat. It's about seven inches long, a perfect model of a sea-going naomhóg, with oars, rowlocks, rudder and mast. And it has seats for eighteen companions, nine rowing on each side.

That boat was found in 1896, ploughed up from a field by a farmer called Tom Nicholl. It's part of a hoard of gold objects that were lost, or placed, close to an ancient shoreline, at the entrance to a lake. When it was turned out of the earth it was crushed by the plough. But now its hollow hull, eggshell-thin, curves again round airy emptiness, and the narrow seats span the hull, waiting for voyagers.

Among the oars and objects found with the boat is one I saw as a slender, gold spear. It's a sensible weapon to take on a journey if you're hunting whales for food. It's also the symbol of Lugh, the sun-god, father of light. As a child I thought the boat was a toy. But I know now that it's an ark. Some Iron Age craftsman or woman, moved by the numinous presence of sea and sky, imagined and shaped it in incorruptible gold as an offering to Manannán, the sea-god. And today, perfect and enigmatic in its glass case in the museum, it still holds everything it was formed to enclose. Lugh's spear of light is an image of truth piercing the darkness of ignorance, and day's return after night.

~~~~

After Ray's death Alice had wanted to stay somewhere peaceful and relaxing that wasn't haunted by the memory of the time we'd all spent here together. Thanks to Mary Curran's suggestion, we found everything she needed at Gorman's; it was a healing place. Most of all we found Síle and Vincent's hospitality. From that first evening, when Wilf and I sat in the garden with Alice, watching the sunset, Síle and Vincent became our friends. Like me, Síle has no roots in Corca Dhuibhne. She first came here at sixteen and fell in love with it. But, unlike me, she never turned aside from the place that had her heart. Instead, she went home after her first visit here knowing exactly what she wanted. And when she was nineteen she packed her bags and came to live here.

She says it never occurred to her to do anything else, though that was a time when there was hardly any work here, and everyone seemed to be leaving for England or America. A year later she married Vincent, whose people have been farmers and fishermen for seven generations. When Síle and Vincent married, John Gorman, Vincent's father, gave them a plot of land across the fields from the family home. During our holiday with Alice I heard how they built their own first home on that plot, a small house facing the ocean with its back to Mount Brandon. The guesthouse Síle welcomed us to is built on the same site. Beyond its front garden, with its edging of lilies and thick clumps of purple chives, a clifftop road curves around the headland. Across the road, the view of the western ocean is encircled by the curving arms of the wide harbour that stretches between the peak called Binn Diarmada and the island called The Black Rock.

To begin with, Vincent continued fishing and farming with his father. And Síle opened a café. She laughs now when she remembers it. 'We hadn't a penny. My mother and I sewed cushions and curtains and Vincent made tables and benches out of old timber. We even wove rushes into placemats!' It was a good beginning.

Vincent's family home was a traditional stone cottage in a place called Glaise Beag, which means 'little stream'. The cottage is empty today but the little stream still runs past it, flowing under the road and through rocky fields till it spills down the cliff into the ocean. Síle can remember her mother-in-law baking bread on the turf fire there, the taste of the milk and eggs Vincent brought home from the farm, and the first time she was faced with a catch of fresh fish thrown down on the kitchen table. She revelled in it all. 'Being here was everything I wanted but in those days it was hard to make a living. There were times we thought of going to America ourselves. But we belonged here.'

So they stuck it out through the hard times and soon people coming to the café were asking if she did bed and breakfast. In a few years she was taking in guests and making evening meals. 'And then one thing led to another and we decided to rebuild and open a proper guesthouse.' They'd just finished decorating it when Mary Curran gave me their number and I called Síle from London.

Because we were still working on our own house in London I was fascinated by the way Síle's decorated hers. It's full of vibrant, jewel-bright colours, like splashes of light on the walls. Bright gold, purple, and deep red paints, black slate and varnished wood, deep blue carpets and crisp white linen. In her bedrooms there are woollen throws woven in blues and earthy greens, echoing the colours of earth, sea and sky.

You find the same awareness of nature and colour in Celtic storytelling. In one story, more than a thousand years old, there's a description of a woman wearing a purple cloak of fleece, held with brooches chased with gold. Her hands are 'as white as the snow of one night' and her cheeks as red as foxgloves. Her eyebrows are as black as a beetle's back, her eyes as blue as hyacinths and her lips as red 'as Parthian leather'. Her hair's 'like the flower of the iris in summer or like pure gold after it's been polished.' As I'm writing this now I can see drifts of those golden irises through the window. They flower here each summer in the fields and ditches around Tí

Neillí Mhuiris, though this year they've been tattered by the wind. If you bring them indoors they wither within hours; each year I pick them, convinced that somehow they'll change their nature once I have them in the house. They never do. They belong outside where they've turned their heads to the sun for over a thousand years.

Sitting by Síle's fire, watching firelight and lamplight on her painted walls, I found myself remembering that story and the amber beads and inlaid boxes I'd seen as a child in the museum. Celtic craftsmen and women loved colour. They decorated bronze and gold with red enamel, and combined silver and jet with crystal beads and carved white bone. Gold was curved and hammered to reflect light, and discs of coloured glass and precious stones were outlined in woven copper. Somewhere along the line, the Celts have got linked in people's minds to wishy-washy mysticism. But in fact they were vibrant, argumentative and in love with brilliance and clarity. Here in the pure light of Corca Dhuibhne you can see what inspired them. This place is still full of craftsmen and women. And whether they're builders, stonemasons, weavers, potters or painters, they still respond to the colours and light that surround them.

Louis Mulcahy's one of the most remarkable craftsmen in Ireland. When Wilf and I first came here to Corca Dhuibhne, Louis' workshop, near the beach at a place called Clogher, was among the first places we'd head for.

It's a series of low, white buildings, set into the lower slopes of a mountain called Cruach Mhárthain.

Louis is a potter on a heroic scale. He makes huge, graceful pots glazed in spectacularly beautiful colours which he's developed himself over more than half a lifetime. I remember the first day we arrived at the workshop and found a blaze of orange marigolds and montbretia crowded into deep blue, pale jade, and creamy-grey vases, among stacks of plates, platters and bowls. The colours ranged from deep grass-green to the palest duck-egg blue. There's a wonderful photo of Louis himself, carrying a huge-bellied, open-mouthed jar on his shoulder, emerging from the waves on Clogher beach, wreathed in spray like Manannán rising from the ocean. Coming here over the years Wilf and I would buy a plate or a dish, and as the years passed we watched Louis' colours, shapes and glazes develop and change. His latest works are as brown as the 'black' turf that's still cut here on the mountains, with speckled panels like a thrush's breast.

Louis' people, like my mother's, come from the east of Ireland. His wife Lisbeth, who's a weaver, is Danish. They came to Corca Dhuibhne over forty years ago, raised a family, and have lived and worked here since. On our first visit to Gorman's we ate off Louis' pottery and, chatting to Síle, we found it was Lisbeth who'd helped her to find the vibrant, deeply satisfying colours in her guesthouse. The earth- and ocean-coloured woollen throws in Gorman's bedrooms, and the wall-hangings of abstract images of the mountains, were designed by Lisbeth, who has her own workshop in Dingle. Everything about Louis and Lisbeth's work is powerful and peaceful, echoing Corca Dhuibhne's shapes, colours and light. Lasse, their son, now lives on the slopes of Cruach Mhárthain where he built his own family house, and runs the pottery. It was he who sold us Tí Neillí Mhuiris. Which explains why Wilf stumbled on that broken pot, glazed in smoky bands of purple-grey and speckled aquamarine, the first day he walked round Neillí's garden.

As soon as I saw Tí Neillí Mhuiris I knew we'd found what we'd been looking for. But I didn't realise what else we'd found. In the first weeks of excitement after we'd bought it, Wilf and I were enchanted by visions of the future. I remember fantasising about sitting in sunshine on my own front doorstep, eating a new-laid egg for breakfast and gazing up at the mountain before settling down to work at my computer. There was hard physical work to be done on the house first. At the time, we saw that as just an obstacle to be overcome before the real stuff started. Whereas, in fact, it brought us new joys we'd never anticipated.

Living beyond a mountain range on a narrow peninsula, people here are used to building and making whatever they need. Fishermen traditionally have been boatbuilders, farmers have walled their own fields and built their homes with their own hands. In the past, women spun and wove cloth to supplement the family income. Every housewife knew how to make baskets to strain potatoes and carry turf. Every child learnt to handle tools and, often, how to make them. And each generation has passed practical skills and knowledge onto the next through advice and demonstration.

In Wilf's first months alone here in Tí Neillí Mhuiris, his days took on a rhythm of knackering work broken by neighbourly pauses for chat, inspection and suggestions. It was our first experience of the sheer practicality of communal memory. Jack knew who'd put in the current fireplace, and why the fire would smoke again if we took it out. He knew where every flower and bush had been in the garden. As he got to know Wilf, he lent him tools, and suggested where to get materials. He'd think about a problem for days and then provide the solution. And every word he said was worth listening to. On cold evenings Wilf would sit by the range in the farmhouse kitchen, chatting, learning and watching television. Then, when the weather forecast was over and the prospects for tomorrow's work had been discussed, he'd walk back up the hill, watching the bats and the martins swooping through the dusk, catching insects.

As time went on, word went round and other neighbours came to inspect the work. Mike George, who farms above on the mountain, knew the lie of our land when

Wilf was putting in drains. And when Wilf hit jobs he couldn't manage on his own, or do himself, people would give him introductions. Maria's boyfriend, Jimmy Hand, knew a man who worked on the boats and might have a fitting for a gas hob; later on, Maria sent him to her neighbour, Christy, who had the long-handled rollers needed to paint a boarded ceiling. Lasse texted him a phone number and a genial whirlwind called Billy turned up to replace the roof tiles. Then, when it rained at a crucial point when the tiles were off, Lasse himself arrived in a van and offered to store our mattress.

Billy's another heroic craftsman. He builds solid structures, made to withstand Corca Dhuibhne's Atlantic gales, and he doesn't deal in fancy names on colour charts. I remember showing him some paint once, when Wilf and I were working on the exterior of the house. I was pleased because I'd discovered the exact colour I'd wanted for the bargeboards under the roof. And I thought that, as a roofer, Billy might be interested. He looked into the tin I was stirring with a stick. ''Tis black', he said. 'It's not', I said, 'it's Invisible Green'. He looked at it again, said nothing and climbed up his ladder. Standing in the garden, I watched him gauge the angle of the wind, shifting his weight like a sailor in a ship's rigging, his practised hands transforming the pile of slates beside him into the die-straight roof that protects our house today. Later, as I stood back to admire my paintwork, he passed behind me, on the way to his van. 'See?' I said, happily, 'Invisible Green.' Billy looked up at it. ''Tis black,' he said. 'And 'tis miserable.'

Once, when the roof was nearly done, I saw Wilf investigating the dank, earth-floored space under the bedroom floorboards. Glancing over Wilf's shoulder, Billy reckoned that what we needed was a concrete sub-floor. Wilf knew we did, but it was a huge amount of work, so he'd thought of just opening up the sub-floor ventilation and replacing the floorboards. Billy gave him a look, saw how tired he was, and announced what was going to happen. Three days later he turned up at the house with a cement lorry. It was a brief diversion from another job he was working on. That day, working at incredible speed, Billy and his two sons barrowed three cubic metres of cement through Neilí Mhuiris's front door and created our sub-floor. I remember Billy himself, up to the tops of his Wellingtons in wet cement, wielding a shovel like a hero, as yet another grey, dripping barrow-load was trundled into the house over a bridge of planks, and shot into the deep, plastic-lined pit that's now beneath my bedroom floor. Out of the maelstrom emerged a perfectly level surface. Then he and his sons were gone, as suddenly as they'd appeared. We paid for the cement but they wouldn't take a penny for the labour.

Looking back now, the kindness of people we hardly knew then seems astonishing. But there's a saying here that defines how the community works. *Ar scáth a chéile a maireann na daoine.* It means 'people live in each other's shadows'. When Wilf was here on his own he'd walk to Murphy's pub in Ballyferriter after a day's work, exhausted and filthy. Nora, the bean a' tí, would send him upstairs for a hot shower while his pint was settling on the counter. For weeks, Maria insisted on taking his laundry to put in her washing machine. Síle drove round with snacks and cans of beer and forced him to sit and take breaks in the overgrown garden. Vincent turned up one day with their son, Máirtín, and helped lift an oven that was being a devil to fit. In Corca Dhuibhne, this spontaneous generosity's just being neighbourly, a central part of a traditional way of life. From time to time strangers who come here take advantage of it. But the locals value their heritage more than they fear exploitation. Besides, they can usually see what's coming and take evasive action. They're no fools.

One day in those first months here in Tí Neillí Mhuiris Wilf was looking for fitments for a door. He knew exactly what he wanted; it was a hook and hasp strong enough to hold the door open against the wall of the house and prevent it from banging in the wind. In London there's always a hardware store or a DIY outlet round the corner. But here at the end of the peninsula if you haven't got what you need and you can't find it in a local shop you're faced with a long trip over the mountain. Or several days wait when you've put in an order on the internet. Having failed to find what he wanted locally, Wilf was sitting in Jack's kitchen one night, feeling fed up. He'd done the trip over the mountain once already that week, before he'd realised he needed the fitment, and he didn't want to waste another day when he could be working. When Jack heard the story, he thought for a minute, opened the range door and stirred up the coals with a poker. Then he asked why Wilf wouldn't take his problem to Barry the Smith.

Next day, when I arrived from London, I gave Wilf a warning. To the ancient Celts, all smiths were descended from Goibniu, the smith of the gods. They came next in rank to judges, poets, physicians and priests, and they were believed to have magic powers. In the past, to keep on the right side of them, a master smith was always sent the head of any animal that was roasted for the king's table; and, if he chose, a smith could claim a place at the table himself. In fact, the belief in the smith's power went so deep that it extended across continents and lasted for millennia. In living memory here in Ireland, people feared a smith's curse and went to him for healing. And when animals were killed, the head would still be sent as a gift to the local blacksmith.

After all that it seemed a bit of an anticlimax to turn

up at a forge in a Nissan Micra wanting a hook and hasp. But Jack had told us where to go so we set off in the car next morning with a sketch of what we required. The forge was on the road to Dingle, a beautiful building of dressed stone, with the smith's house beside it. It was built in the nineteenth century as part of the local English landlord's estate and looks slightly out of place in an area where so many buildings were made from uncut field stones. But if its outside looked like a Victorian postcard, the inside felt like a cave.

The smith met us on the threshold. He was a powerful, elderly man, who moved slowly and spoke gently. We explained who we were and who'd sent us and he ushered us inside. As my eyes got used to the dim light I saw a mixture of order and apparent chaos, tools hanging in neat rows on the walls and what seemed to be heaps of metal piled up around an iron furnace. Wilf was fascinated by the mechanism that pumped air through a duct from the next room. I was remembering the belief that just by turning his anvil a smith could tap into the power of Goibniu, the god who made the weapons of the gods that shaped the world.

Wilf described what he needed and we all stepped back out into the sunny yard to look at his sketch. Could it be made for us? 'Of course it could, it was nothing at all,' but the furnace would need to be fired specially. With his shoulders against the wall and his eyes on the distance, he told us it was a long time since the fire was kept up every day. In the past, people had come for miles to him to shoe horses, mend things and make tools. 'You'd make tools for every tradesman one time, and you'd make your own as well.' He listed the tailor's needle and the sailor's anchor, the carpenter's saw and the thatcher's knife; in his own day he'd made spades, pitchforks and scythes, nails, hinges and locks, gates and fire irons, and buckles for harness makers. It was a list I'd known from a book of folklore, but this man was speaking from his own experience. 'There was a time when a smith would put stitches of iron wire in a plate or a platter that a woman would have broken on the floor.' I wondered if people had ever come to him for healing in the old days; I'd read that water from the forge trough, in which the irons were cooled, was a cure for skin disease and warts. He shook his head and laughed when I asked him. But later I heard he'd been a horse doctor who'd often cured animals that were given up for dead. He told us he missed the horses, and the tinkers and travellers who used to trade in them. 'They were good people and they had great skills. And now there's no call for their skills, where are they? Fenced into some campsite, or inside in a council estate, where no one has a civil word to say for them.'

We left him Wilf's sketch and drove off, having arranged to come back the next week. He made us two sets of long hooks and two hasps, all with plates for screws, forged from steel. As I held them in my hand I remembered reading that local forges used to be gathering places. The big doors were used as notice boards, with handbills offering lettings of grazing and auctions of livestock and land. There were always men and boys waiting in line with work to be done, chatting, doing business deals and swapping stories. But when Wilf and I arrived that first day to meet him, there was no one there but the smith; looking back, I know that the work he did for us was done in silence, except for the crackle of flames and the sound of the hammer on the anvil. Like a druid, or like Goibniu, the master-smith of the gods, he would have been alone with his mystery. After the bustling life he'd known the emptiness must have seemed strange. I wish I'd seen him at work by the red-hot furnace. And I wish we'd had something more worthy to ask of his skill than a hook to hold back a door.

But maybe I'm wrong to wish that. My own trade is crafting the world into words, and I know that the shortest sentence must be shaped with the same skill and concentration as the longest one, sometimes even more. I know too that a craftsman absorbed in an act of creation never feels he's alone.

One day that year, when we'd driven a carload of stuff over from London, Jack arrived in Tí Neilli Mhuiris with

the dogs at his heels. There were bags and boxes everywhere and piles of stuff still loaded in the car. Feeling
frazzled after an exhausting trip, I staggered in under
another load of possessions, dumped them on a table
and announced that I hoped to goodness we had everything we needed. The dogs stretched out in a sunny patch
on the floor. Jack sat on a box. 'You have four walls and
a good roof,' he said, 'you have food and a fire, and good
neighbours. You have all you need.'

So I made tea and sat down. I watched Spot's glossy
flank rising and falling to the slow rhythm of her
breathing. And I remembered a story that's told here
about a good roof. An islander called Mike Sé moved
from the Blasket Islands to the mainland. He built the
walls of his new house with field stones. But the roof
beams came with him from his old house on the island.
He rowed them across himself in a naomhóg, and the
neighbours helped him carry them up the cliff. Then,
over his new house here on the mainland he raised the
same roof beams that had sheltered his island home.
'Why wouldn't he?', said the neighbours. 'It was a good
roof.' Those beams still protect that house today, as firm
as the beams Billy found under the tiles he replaced for
us on Tí Neillí Mhuiris.

The men who built Neillí's roof cut the beams by hand
and raised them with ropes. It was done under the same
government scheme that built the slipway out on the

island. Maybe it was overseen by the man who posed in the photo with the watch chain and the hat. I suppose there was cursing and singing, and the neighbours must have come in to lend a hand. The ceiling's made of boards nailed onto the roof beams. The boards run between the two gable ends, slanting in from the front and back walls to a flat, central panel a few feet below the ridge. Wilf and Christy Corduff painted them blue-black, Christy working with the long roller and Wilf working off a ladder, cutting-in between the boards. Last night, during the storm, that dark ceiling seemed to hang in the air above my bed like the hull of an upturned timber boat.

When Wilf removed the partitions and stripped the panelling from the walls, we were left with a wide room with a stone floor, the high blue-black ceiling and creamy-white plaster walls. The fireplace in the north gable end is creamy-white too, though now it's grey-brown as well, where the smoke's touched the edges round the fire. Over it, there's a wide dark shelf that wraps around the chimney piece. Wilf made it out of boards. He took down the timber wall that divided Neillís' two tiny bedrooms from the rest of the house, and built it up again to make one larger bedroom against the south gable end, and a narrow space by the front window for my desk. The desk's made from the top of a table that Lasse and Emer left in the house. It's dark brown and solid and flooded with light from the window at my left shoulder. The timber wall's a deep cream colour on the side that faces into the room, and pale grey in the bedroom. The foot-deep timber windowsills are painted grey as slate.

I love the vibrancy of Corca Dhuibhne's colours and the brilliance of its light. And at first we tried introducing wine-red, purple, and deep russet into the rooms here in Tí Neillí Mhuiris. But we kept repainting them in calmer, gentler colours, and the house became increasingly quiet and more empty. Like the gold boat in its glass case in the museum that I loved as a child, there's a quality of expectation about it. And it seems to me now that we made it as it is because, like the boat, it exists as an ark. Held here between the walls and under the roof, is a space in which life happens moment by moment, and the moments that matter are preserved in memory. Colour comes in with the neighbours round the fire, lamplight and flames, laughter and memories, tunes and songs, the food and drink and the sharing.

Last night, when the wind died down, I slept deeply. After I got up this morning Jack and the dogs came by with a cabbage, on their way up to the cows. I showered and started writing. I drank tea and checked emails, wrote some more, and made a loaf of bread. Outside, the hedges were full of birdsong, and the sun shone on fields of golden irises, tattered by wind and rain. Wilf and I walked on the beach; two men were driving a jeep along the tideline, picking up scallops after the night of storm. After lunch, I walked up the road and picked foxgloves. Then I came back to my desk and wrote again. And all the time a little gold boat, eggshell-thin, its hull curved round airy emptiness, was waiting for the voyagers who would need its spear of light.

8

A Good Floor for Dancing

There's a story here about one of the Blasket
Islands. They say that a herdsman's family was
staying there some time in the nineteenth
century, looking after stock. And one night the old
woman woke up in bed and heard music. At first she
thought she was mistaken and she tried to go to sleep
again. But all the time the sound of the music was getting
nearer, till it was all around the house. So she woke the
old man beside her and they both listened. They couldn't
tell if it was voices or a fiddle they heard, but they knew
it was a lament. All night long it passed away to the cliffs

and back again, coming and going over the house. And the old people lay in the bed, listening. And when the sun rose the music passed away altogether, drifting over the western sea. The old man had a fiddle and he picked out the tune he'd heard, note by note. And he played it till he had it in his hands as well as his head. That tune has stayed with the islanders through generations. The name they gave it was *Port na bPúcaí*, which means 'The Fairy Music'. And the old people said it was a fairy funeral they'd heard, and the sound of lamentation, as one of the fairies was carried to the island for burial, or on across the sea to the Isle of the Blessed.

Máire Begley played 'Port na bPúcaí' here in Tí Neillí Mhuiris, one night in winter when the fire was lit and the tunes had been flying for hours. In a quiet moment, when the music had turned to chat, someone called for Máire to play, and she lifted her piano accordion. Máire's a virtuoso performer, so people hushed each other as she settled the straps on her shoulders and sat forward on her chair. Then she closed her eyes and started to play. No one stirred. I closed my own eyes and listened to the deep notes and complex harmonies rolling between the stone walls and the timber ceiling. Then, with a conscious effort, I opened my eyes again and looked round. The only movements in the room were Máire's hands on the keys and the push and pull of the instrument's bellows. There was no sound but the tune. And from the youngest to the oldest, everyone round me sat with eyes closed and faces raised, breathing to the slow, strong pulse of the music.

Wilf and I first met Máire Begley on a Monday night in the house where her own neighbours used to drop in for evenings of bothántaíocht. I remember it was high summer and Louis Mulcahy, who's a fine singer as well as a potter, drove us there along roads that were blazing with fuchsia. He'd promised we wouldn't be urged to sing or play if we didn't want to. Which was just as well, because I can do neither and Wilf had only just started on the concertina. Music's been in Máire's family for generations. She's a friend now, but then we just knew her as a legend. And that night neither of us quite believed Louis' promise. So we were nervous when we arrived.

On summer evenings at Máire's the half-door was always open. I remember daylight filtering into the room through tall, green stalks of fennel that grew under the low windowsills. Outside the house, the yellow fennel flowers touched the edge of the sloping thatched roof. Inside, the shadowy room was warmed by a glowing turf fire. On the wide hearth was an abstract image of seven rays of light, depicted in tiny stones gathered from the nearby beach. It's said that a local woman, whose name was Mary Margaret, had a vision of seven rays of light round Christ's head, bringing strength to the world. So the stones were set into the hearth when the house was built, to bless the hands that cooked there on the fire.

When Louis led us in that night, I noticed how the floor sloped from the fire towards the door. The floor in Tí Neillí Mhuiris has the same slope. They were both made to be cleaned by throwing water on the hearth and sweeping it down through the house and out into the yard. At Máire's there was a half-loft bedroom, reached by a narrow, wooden staircase, and a second bedroom under it, behind the kitchen. When Wilf was working on Tí Neillí Mhuiris he thought he might find signs that we'd once had a half-loft ourselves. But Tí Neillí Mhuiris was built later than Máire's, and it never seems to have had one. He did find a handmade bench and a stool that must have belonged to Neillí and Paddy. But they'd been in the damp byre for years, and they fell to pieces when he lifted them. Against the wall at Máire's there's a dresser made from planks thrown onto the beach nearly a hundred years ago, by the Atlantic waves. I envy her that dresser, and her chairs that have seats of straw or rye rope, called *súgán*. Some of them have always been there. Others she's collected. Some, with three legs, were made to stand on the uneven earth floors that, until about fifty years ago, were common in most houses on the peninsula. They were sawn and planed and pegged together by hand. Over the years they've gained thick layers of paint; cream, muddy brown, grass green, and red ochre.

There's a sixteenth-century hymn in Irish that's still played in Corca Dhuibhne today. It's called 'Big Mary is A Good Woman'. The words describe the Celtic Christian image of Christ's mother. She's no meek maiden with downcast eyes. Instead she's Big Mary who puts her cloak around the world. Like the Good Goddess, she's the 'strongest and most energetic of women' the destroyer of her children's enemies and a powerful shield in battle. Máire is the Irish form of Mary, and I first heard that tune played in Máire Begley's house. Maybe that's why I think of Máire as Big Mary. She's creative, energetic and big-hearted. Music's her family inheritance, and with it comes a duty to pass it on. Everyone comes to her music nights, from professional musicians to kids with tin whistles. She's a professional herself, and her hospitality and currant cakes are famous, so latecomers often have to stand in the doorway while the people inside cram onto benches and the kids sit on the stairs.

Mondays at Máire's are gatherings of generations, continuing the tradition that's survived here for thousands of years. They're also great nights out. Máire's a traditional harpist. She's a virtuoso on the accordion, bringing the intricate, West Kerry style to jigs and hornpipes, polkas and slides. But she's just as likely to swing into a medley of hot jazz standards on piano. That first night, sitting in the shadows at the back of the room, I watched her welcoming friends and strangers, making sure everyone was heard and encouraging the youngest, shyest performers to bring what they could to the evening's entertainment. It's a lesson to see how everyone benefits when each contribution gets the same attention and respect.

As time passed and we gained more courage, Wilf and I would arrive at Máire's on our own. We'd lift the latch on darker, winter evenings in the season of Samhain, to find the room lit by lamplight and candlelight, and flames leaping on the hearth. Fennel flowers powder away in drifts of yellow dust in winter, leaving skeletal, silver seed pods on bleached stalks like bones. The dead stalks pull easily from the earth and their faint, spicy smell mixes with the rich smell of black turf when they're thrown on the fire. Those smells are always in the background at Máire's, along with the warm smells of currant cake and fresh bread. On winter nights the wind blows rain so fiercely against the windows it seems that they must break. Draughts sweep under the half-door. The warmth and companionship keep out the chill of the night, but people still jostle discreetly for seats near the fire, and players warm cold fingers round hot mugs of tea. Then, in early spring, comes the season the Celts called Imbolc. I remember the first day I walked from our car to Máire's door and felt the change in the air. In the deep beds under the windowsills the dormant fennel was starting to stir.

You never know who you'll meet at Máire's. One night Wilf was mildly surprised to see a well-known English operatic tenor amble in with a neighbour from down the road. He and the singer had worked together so, when Máire brought in the tea, they chatted about mutual friends in London and Paris, sitting on súgán chairs with their mugs balanced on their knees. Later on, from a seat by the door, the singer stunned the room into silence with a Mozart aria that rattled the china on the dresser. He was followed by Lil, aged eighty-one, who sang an emigrant's lament in a sweet, thread-like voice from her rocking chair by the fire.

On another night a teenager from Israel turned up with some local girls. Máire asked if he'd a song or a tune and he shook his head. He obviously felt shy and I felt for him, remembering our own first night there. But by then I knew Máire, so I knew he'd be fine. She gave him a smile, turned away, and the evening went on. But later on, still looking away from him, she sidled into *Hava Nagila* on the accordion. People started clapping, slowly at first and then faster. Then three neighbours, who'd been dancing a jig earlier, couldn't stay in their seats. And within minutes the shy boy found himself in front of a turf fire, happily leading a circle of middle-aged Irishwomen through a dance he hadn't tried since his Bar Mitzvah.

We had our first party here in Tí Neillí Mhuiris before we met Máire. It started as a housewarming to thank the people who'd helped us since we'd arrived. We weren't sure who'd want, or have time, to come. But we wanted to invite everyone who'd been so generous and welcoming. So invitations went up the hill, to Mike and Jim George and their families, and down the hill, to Jack and Mrs Manning and Jimmy and Maria. We left messages on answerphones, sent texts and flagged down cars, asking the neighbours to pass on the word of a party in Tí Neillí Mhuiris. Then we drove to Ventry, where Jim Long keeps the village shop and post office, and put in an order for bread and ham for sandwiches, tea, coffee, wine and milk. Then we went to Dingle and got sherry, beers and whiskey for the die-hards. Later, while I was making scones, Wilf sneaked out to visit the woman who baked for the local museum café in Ballyferriter. We'd planned the house-warming for the weekend of my birthday, so he'd decided to order a cake.

It was a sunny evening in August. I'd made stacks of sandwiches. The fire was lit but the windows and door were open. There were chairs in the garden as well as in the house, though everything outside was still a bit wild and uncared for. Onions, potatoes, parsnips and turnips flourished in the die-straight ridges. But all around them the waving meadow grass had reasserted itself, and wild roses rambled through the hedges. Con's arbutus was still smothered. Paddy's nettles were making a comeback. But we slashed and stamped out a flat patch among purple clover and towering thistles, and set out upturned boxes for seats and a table. I made yet more sandwiches. Then we walked down to Jack's to borrow his bench.

It's a wooden bench he built himself, painted red-brown and made to fit tidily along the stretcher under his kitchen table. When we arrived he lifted out the bench and stood it up against the wall. We chatted a while, and talked to the dogs. Then Wilf and I walked back up the hill, carrying the bench between us. I remember wondering if a party in high summer was really a good idea if most of your guests are farmers, fishermen, or working in tourism. Then we rounded the corner and found a huge, dripping bag of crab claws hanging from a tree beside the gate. By that point we were slightly more in tune with things than we'd been when we found the seaweed. So, putting two and two together, we called Maria. It was the right call. Jimmy couldn't make the party because he had to go fishing. So he'd left a contribution to the feast.

Those crab claws and that bench made the party. After we found the bag on the tree we walked back down to Jack's and borrowed a huge saucepan. Then we drove to the post office again and bought serious quantities of butter. Then Wilf went out to the shed for a couple of hammers. And we were good to go.

When I look back on that night, I see it as the final turning point on a road I'd been travelling since I first took the boat to England. I'd spent so many years longing to get back to Corca Dhuibhne. Wilf and I had used it for so long as an escape. I knew what I loved about the place itself. The high clouds. The changing seasons. The steel grey, jade and turquoise ocean. Wings whirring in the hedgerows. The cows swaying heavily down long rutted lanes. And the constant presence of the mountain. What I didn't know yet was what it means to live here as part of the community.

It was the final turning point, but it wasn't dramatic. It was just the beginning of a new process that's gone on ever since. That night the neighbours drifted in bringing food and drink and offers of help in the kitchen. Actually, I'm wrong. They didn't offer. They just did things. At some point, I went in for a bottle opener and found Maria's twelve-year-old sister at the sink. She waved a dismissive hand at me and plunged another glass into the soapsuds. 'You', she said, 'go back out.' So I did. Back in the room, I found Jack's bench had been placed in front of the fire. Jim George helped Wilf to drain the boiling crab claws, and the hot pan was set on a bread board on the bench. Jack, who'd walked up with Spot, had been sitting by the wall. As soon as the pan hit the bread board, someone gave him a hammer and he was astride the bench. And for the next twenty minutes the room was a riot of smashing shells, flying shards and dripping, melted butter. It was the most luscious, tender crabmeat I'd ever tasted, sucked straight from the coral pink, black-tipped claws. Someone handed me a share, and I sat in a corner with Spot. I'd suddenly realised this wasn't my party. It wasn't even our party. It belonged to everyone who'd come here to enjoy themselves. No complicated work relationships. No networking. No guilt about failing to network. No need to do anything but enjoy myself as well.

So I sat there, looking and listening. The room was full of voices, speaking Irish and English. Sometimes a conversation would flow from one language to the other with no sense of change. Christy Corduff's wife, Cathy, arrived with a huge cream-filled pavlova, studded with summer fruit. I could see Christy on the other side of the room, talking to Wilf. They were craning their necks at the ceiling and discussing a series of inexplicable dents they'd noticed in some of the boards when they'd painted it. They still couldn't explain them. Carmel, Jim George's wife, doesn't like crabmeat, so she'd opted for ham sandwiches. She was sitting by the door, talking to Mike George's wife, Mary. Mike George and his cousin Breandán 'ac Gearailt were discussing the view from our back window, which looks up towards their village up the mountain. Maria's dad, Mikeen, was sitting by the fire, smoking his pipe. He was a watcher too. His dark face was like a hawk's and his eyes were narrow slits, gleaming like glass. Louis and Lisbeth arrived with Lasse, Emer and Líobhán. They brought flowers. I watched Wilf dividing them between several pint glasses, because we hadn't got a vase. Later, I found they'd been transferred to a bucket in the kitchen, because we hadn't enough glasses. Later still, I found them carefully laid in a sinkful of water, because someone had used the bucket and mop to wash the floor.

Sitting there in my corner, I found Spot staring longingly at the crab claws I was eating from a saucer. I offered her one. With a guilty glance at Jack, who was still wielding the hammer, she took it neatly in her mouth and vanished into the garden. Through the open window I could hear kids, bored with sitting indoors, playing football in the road. The mountain glowed purple in the dusk. I could see cigarette tips glowing too, where smokers sat on upturned boxes in the garden. I could hear Jack's nephew, Terry, and Ken from down the road, chatting as they leaned against the front wall with bottles of beer in their hands. Someone handed out a bowl of crab claws followed by white pepper and a lump of yellow butter in a dish. Terry moved across the grass towards the makeshift table, and Spot circled the smokers, hopefully licking her lips.

Later still, when the pavlova and the birthday cake were eaten, Wilf – fortified by drink – got up to sing. When we'd planned the party we'd hoped there might be music. But it hadn't seemed fair to expect our guests to lead the way. Back then there was no keyboard in the house, and

Cliodhna was yet to climb the hill with her concertina. So Wilf had no choice but to start with a song. It was just a series of doggerel verses set to an old tune, with a repeated chorus. I'd written it that afternoon. There's a tradition here of making songs and poems to mark particular occasions, or to describe local characters and events. My song described Christy painting the ceiling, and Billy doing the roof, Nora letting Wilf take showers, and Maria washing his socks. Most people in the room could probably have done it better. But they laughed and clapped, and recognised that, despite the drink, Wilf was shaking with nerves as he sang it. So everyone joined in the chorus.

There was an awkward moment after the clapping died down. Then Mikeen, by the fire, grabbed Wilf's hand and launched into a song of his own. It was a generous gesture, recognising what we were trying to do and helping it along. He had a voice like a creaky gate and everyone loved it. When he finished there was another burst of laughter and applause. I held my breath, wondering what would happen next, wishing I had something more to offer myself. And then, sitting by the open window, Louis suddenly began to sing. From my corner in the room, I watched the circle of glowing cigarette tips in the garden grow nearer, drawn by his voice. The song was English, though he sang with his head bent and his hands between his knees, almost like a sean-nós singer. Outside, the glowing cigarette tips gathered round the open window like fireflies. During the applause that followed the song, Breandán 'ac Gearailt slipped out the door to his car and came back with an instrument case. Perched on the edge of a chair, he took out an old, well-played button accordion. And the dancing began.

I remember Louis and Lisbeth whirling round the room, missing teacups by inches. Jack waltzing. And Cathy Corduff shimmying across the floor with a tottering pile of plates. And I remember Breandán himself, still playing the accordion, dancing across the room and stamping his foot. It looked like a solo interlude, but actually he'd spotted a beetle crawling in from the garden and had neatly killed it off. At some point Aoileann, Breandán's wife, produced a flute. They played on together, one instrument complementing the other. And then, when the dancing was over, Breandán stood by the fire and began to remember.

As he talked, the people in the room seemed to slip out of focus and echoes of other, older gatherings began to take their place. He talked about Neillí and Paddy, and the dog that used to sit up at the table when they were eating. He pointed to where they'd sat, and to where his own father and the other neighbours sat when they used to visit here. He talked about Paddy's fear that the wind from the mountain would lift the roof, and about the whiskey bottle in the two-pound marmalade jar he'd used to predict the weather. He showed us the windowsill where it had stood. And people nodded, remembering. Mike's Mary remembered the tin of biscuits Neillí kept under the bed. Jim George had been sent down to the post office as a child to collect Paddy and Neillí's pensions. When he'd run into the smoky house with the money, he couldn't see the fireplace from the door. Then Breandán named the neighbours who'd sat here down the years. 'Paidí 'n Mháma. Bobbí' 'n Rí. John Tommí, Davy Jeaic. Mike Sheáin-Cavin. Gugail. John Micí. Toní and Johneen.' The names rolled out like a litany. And people nodded, remembering. He pointed to the corner where the calf used to be tied beside the dresser. He remembered neighbours' kids playing tricks on Paddy, telling him they'd heard storm warnings on the radio. He remembered nights when it was mostly men who'd gather here, and how Neillí would sit by the fire and wonder at their stories. Paddy had tales of boxing matches and adventures in America, and of hunting hares here on the mountain, above the house. Neillí would raise her hands in astonishment as she listened. '*Céad míle glóir' le Dia!*', she'd say. 'A hundred thousand glories to God!'

Then Breandán talked about music. I'd already heard about Neillí's own songs, about the rent man and the cost of food, and life in this house where her door was always open and our own neighbours now had come to visit. Now I was hearing about Breandán's father, Jeaic, and the songs he'd sung here. And how Seán de hÓra, one of the most famous sean-nós singers of his time, was a cousin of Paddy's, and used to cross the Clasach to visit him from his own house in Dún Chaoin. And that the composer Seán Ó Ríada, who came to Dún Chaoin to learn from Seán de hÓra, used to wander in as well. The same roof and walls that echoed with their voices, holds the music that's played here today. In Irish traditional music terms, it was like hearing that John Lennon used to hang out in your house picking up tips from Frank Sinatra. As Breandán's list of names went on I felt like throwing my own hands up in wonder. He spoke of fiddles and pipes and long nights of singing and dancing. But I suppose it wasn't really that surprising. Corca Dhuibhne's always been a place for music. And Tí Neillí Mhuiris was always a great house for bothántaíocht.

It's hard to find anyone in Corca Dhuibhne who can't knock a tune out of a tin whistle or stand up for a dance down the pub. But particular families here, like Máire Begley's, have always been known for their music. 'Port na bPúcaí' was first recorded in the 1960s, played by a man called Seán Cheaist Ó Catháin, who was born on the Great Blasket. Years later it was recorded again, by his granddaughter, Áine Cheaist Uí Laoithe. Like Eilín Ní Chearna, who often plays and sings with her, Áine's known as an island woman, though their families came out to the mainland before Áine or Eilín were born. Like Máire Begley, they're musicians whose presence fills a pub. You hear they're going to be there and the texts start flying. The music they've inherited still passes down through their families. And, like Máire, they're also teachers, eager to share their stories.

When Wilf started on the concertina he taught himself, working out the fingering and finding the notes and chords. When Neillí and Paddy died, the field above the garden here went to Seán de hÓra; I remember his widow's cows standing in a straight line along the hedge as Wilf sat out in the garden, struggling to find a tune. Cows are like that. I don't think they're particularly interested in music. They gather with the same grave attention no matter what's going on.

After that first party we had others, not so big or formal, more like nights of bothántaíocht. They became part of the rhythm of our years. We'd pass the word that the fire was lit and neighbours would just ramble in and chat. One night, talking to Carmel, I heard that while Wilf and the cows were getting to grips with the concertina, Jim and Carmel's nine-year-old son, Seán, had been learning the accordion from Máire Begley's brother, Breanndán. (Identification always needs to be specific here, because you get a lot of people with the same names and surnames. That's why Neillí was identified by her father's name, Muiris, and Jim and his brother Mike, whose surname is Mac Gearailt, are usually known by their father's name, George. Incidentally, the reason Muiris becomes Mhuiris has to do with the complexity of Irish grammar. And the complexity of Irish grammar's one reason why, ten years later, Wilf's learnt the concertina, but has yet to learn the language.) Anyway, the next night, Seán Jim George came down with his mum and dad and played some tunes he'd learnt from Breanndán Begley. And Wilf joined in on the concertina. Then we went up the mountain to Jim and Carmel's a few nights later, and had some tunes up there. Winter's the time for bothán-taíocht, when fires are lit and the nights are dark, and the harvest of the summer months is gathered in. I remember frosty nights walking down from Jim and Carmel's, carrying Wilf's concertina case, with a huge starry sky above us and lights shining in windows all round the valley below.

Then, the following spring, Carmel rang to say Seán was going to *Scoil Cheoil an Earraigh*, and did Wilf want to go with him? When I translated, Wilf wasn't sure. But it seemed that the neighbours had decided for him. It was the general feeling that, where the concertina was concerned, he'd gone as far he was going to on his own.

Scoil Cheoil an Earraigh means 'the Spring Music School'. It was set up in Ballyferriter by Breanndán Begley and Níamh Ní Bhaoill. Breanndán's another virtuoso performer with music in his blood. Níamh, who was raised in Connemara, raised her own family here in Corca Dhuibhne. Her television production company makes music documentaries for Irish-language television, and she plays a mean tin whistle herself.

As long as I've been coming to Corca Dhuibhne I've heard discussions about how changing customs are changing the way that traditional music's shared. Now, when everything's globally accessible and often shared through video and sound files, individual styles belonging to particular places can easily be lost. Which means that levels of richness and specificity in Corca Dhuibhne's centuries-old tradition could disappear. That was why Níamh and Breanndán chose three days in February, when the primary school in Ballyferriter's closed for half-term, and started a music event that now takes over the village every spring.

In the first year there were just seven classes. Last year it was twenty-seven, with extra teachers for some instruments because of the numbers of students that wanted to come. Over the years Níamh and Breanndán have added talks, local history walks and Irish lessons. But music classes, sessions, dancing and concerts are still the heart of the school. It's about the genuine, native, West Kerry style. Everything happens in Irish. Each available room in the village gets taken over, including the school, the pubs, the café and the local museum. There are classes on the harp, fiddle, accordion, bodhrán, banjo and mandolin, pipes, flute, mouth organ and concertina. There's set dancing and step dancing. And at night there are concerts in the village hall over near Síle's, with line-ups of traditional musicians that bring audiences from Europe and America, as well as from all over Ireland.

Carmel says she wishes she'd had a camera to catch Wilf and Seán as they went down the hill that year – nine-year-old Seán with his huge accordion, and gangling Wilf with his little concertina box. As Wilf left the house I suspected he was a bit daunted by the idea of classes through Irish, not to mention the challenge of playing with musicians who'd been steeped in traditional music since they were born. Later on he told me he'd been terrified. The village was crowded with people carrying instrument cases, queuing in the school hall to register, scuttling round trying to find their classrooms and grabbing scones and coffee in the pubs. Seán brought Wilf into the school to sign up for concertina classes with Breanndán's son, Cormac Begley. Then he registered for his own class and was gone. Eventually, Wilf found himself sitting in a circle with a dour middle-aged man from Cork, three frighteningly competent ten-year-old girls and Cormac, whose skill and speed on the concertina are extraordinary; it was a baptism of fire but he loved it. And, most of the time, he followed what Cormac was saying. I suppose that when words didn't work they fell back on the music.

On the last morning of each Scoil Cheoil there's a

students' concert. Sometimes musicians from the evening concerts will turn up and play along. These days there are so many students that the concert happens in the village church. But in Wilf's first year it was in the village school. Carmel and I went in together. Crowded into the biggest classroom, with kids' paintings and projects on the walls, were students of all ages. There were farmers from the hills and kids down from Dublin. There were Bretons and Americans. There were two members of The Chieftains, who'd topped the bill at the concert the night before. Somehow they'd ended up on a couple of titchy school chairs, leaving their knees on a level with their ears.

I was sitting on a pile of tables in the corner as Breanndán Begley waded through the crowd with his accordion, calling for order. The crowd settled down. Over the heads I could see Áine Cheaist holding out her hand to her first sean-nós student. He sang. In between verses there were traditional murmurs of appreciation and encouragement, and he sat down to cheers and applause. The classes in each instrument played separately, led by their teachers. Then the whole lot played together. It was a West Kerry polka, called 'We Won't Go Home Till Morning'. Somewhere in the middle, perched on titchy school chairs, Seán and his accordion, Wilf and his concertina, and the two members of The Chieftains were happily playing along. After the concert there was music outside every pub in the village, and dancing in the road. And that night, the sessions in the pubs went on till dawn.

Nights at Máire Begley's, and those first classes at Scoil Cheoil an Earraigh, were the next step on the road for Wilf as a musician. They introduced him to Níamh and Breanndán and to his friend Maidhc, whom he met at Cormac's class the following year. Maidhc's a farmer and fisherman, a student of folklore and a teacher of Irish. It was his wife, Ann, who had the concertina, but one day Maidhc picked it up; it must have felt right in his hand because he's played it ever since. It took time for Wilf to find the courage to play in the pubs but, when the time came a year or so later, it was Maidhc who introduced him to the sessions he still plays in now in the village.

They're easy quiet evenings by the pub fire, led by Bríd Donnelly, a flute player and a generous teacher with an encyclopedic memory for tunes and for who played which version of them. Friends ramble in one after the other, choose a table and wander over to the bar to order drinks. Texts have gone round to the usual neighbours. But you never quite know who'll turn up. Maidhc. Aideen, a gardener, who works in a bookshop in Dingle and plays the fiddle. Níamh. Or Máire Malone, who's a local schoolteacher. Instrument cases are left on the floor, mobiles on the table and bags slung over chairs. 'Aon scéal?' they'll ask, and chat with the neighbours at the bar. The kettle's boiled to make tea and coffee while the pints are being poured. Nothing's hurried. Glasses are tipped at the correct angle and the dark pints are left to rest till they're properly settled and topped up. Everyone knows you can't rush a good pint; anything worth having is worth waiting for.

As I write this now I can hear Wilf outside playing a polka. It's a long time since he graduated from playing to the cows. The tune's called 'Polca Sheáin Mhaidhc', and he composed it as a gift for Ann and Maidhc's newborn son.

Maidhc's family have lived here for generations. Like many men from Corca Dhuibhne, he worked in America for a while. But he came home to farming and fishing and his son will grow up in the house he and Ann have built here, looking over the ocean. The first day we visited baby Seán Mhaidhc he was asleep in a wooden cradle, built by his dad. So when we came home Wilf wrote another polka, called 'Making the Cradle'. Then he wrote a third, called 'Polca Hanna', for Terry and Cliodhna's daughter, who was born in the same month. Traditional tunes are always played in threes. And music has always played its part here in preserving memories.

When I started to write this chapter I remembered a story I heard years ago about a fiddle on the island, made of *reac*. Reac's what people here call anything useful that the ocean throws onto the shore. Even now, after a storm people will walk the beaches, looking to see what they can find. In the past everything the ocean provided was used, and used again. Objects that were found then, and things that were made from reac, are now treasured as heirlooms. The dresser at Máire Begley's was made of planks from the beach, carefully gathered, dried, sorted and saved till the man who found them had enough to build what he needed. Reac was particularly important to the islanders because every piece of wood they had came from the ocean. Each was found on a beach by someone who'd watched and waited patiently, knowing the tides and the seasons that would bring it to his hand. Driftwood was precious. So were the wreckage and cargoes of lost ships, some of which saved the islanders' lives in times of famine. Every man, woman and child who lived there must have been watching out for reac on every tide. And one man watched with a head full of music. He was waiting for the makings of a fiddle. 'And did the reac come?' I asked the man who told me the story. 'It did,' he said. And the fiddle was made, and played for long years after. He had a notion that someone had it still.

I remembered that story again last night when Wilf and I were at a session in the village. There was a pause in the music while people chatted and went for drinks. The day had been fine but the month has been wet; so people talked about their crops, and how the north wind had burnt the leaves on the ash trees. In a lull in the chat I asked about the island fiddle, 'was it really made from reac?' Bríd said she remembered hearing about it. Other people joined in. 'Wasn't there that gathering a few years ago to celebrate the island music? Didn't someone restore it then, and they played it?' As we talked, Máire Malone, who'd been to the bar, came back with a pint and sat down. When she heard what I'd asked about she laughed. 'Sure, it wasn't only on the island. Back west they all made fiddles. And other instruments. I heard of them myself back in Emlagh.' She settled her pint on the table by her whistle. 'Sure they had to make them, girl, if they hadn't the money to buy them. They had to have music.'

I left the session at eleven-thirty. As I passed the pub window I could see them still sitting round the table. When I'd stood up to go they'd stopped for a break. People were talking and checking mobiles. Aideen and Bríd had their heads together, tuning their fiddles. People sipped drinks and coffee. Then someone started a tune on a whistle, another whistle picked it up, and the rest of the players joined in. I could still hear the music as I walked the steep road towards the house. It was a windless night in mid-June, with light still in the sky. The road bends sharply above the village and, looking back, I could see the houses below, and the luminous ocean beyond. The sky was pale grey tinged with purple, and faintly streaked with pink. The curving mass of the headland was charcoal black edged with silver. The deep, rhythmic sound of the waves hid the faint sound of the music below in the village. Closer by, in fields on either side of me, I could hear cows shifting and breathing. Now and then I heard the precise, crunching, tearing sound of their jaws closing on grass. Along the centre of the road a strip of grass had broken through the tarred surface, seeded by birds and the droppings of cattle and sheep. In the pale light, meadowsweet and honeysuckle glowed beside me in the ditches. The higher I climbed, the more the rhythmic sound of the sea and the deep breathing of the creatures filled the air around me.

I remember an evening at Máire Begley's own house, when she played 'Port na bPúcaí'. There were kids sitting on the stairs, peering down through the wooden banisters. Firelight played on the seven rays of stone light embedded in the hearth. People closed their eyes. As the deep notes and complex harmonies filled the shadowy room, no one stirred but eighty-one-year-old Lil. With her head bent, and her hands linked in her lap, she sat rocking in her chair beside the fire.

When the tune was played, Máire told the story of the old people on the island who listened all night to the fairy music that echoed round their house. And then she told another story, to cap it. Fishermen here say that when a school of humpback whales passes under a canvas boat, whale song can reverberate through the hull. So maybe, she said, there were whales in the ocean that night, as the old people lay in bed listening. And maybe it was whale song, echoing up through folds and crevasses in the cliffs, that filled the air round the herdsman's house with music.

9

Who You Are Is Where You Come From

Identity matters in Ireland. When people meet, they try to place each other, and they're not happy till they find links that join their story to yours. They want to know where you come from. If they can, they'll find they're related to you. But they'll settle for knowing you were born a couple of roads from their mother's cousin, or that you use the same broadband provider, or your best friend owns a caravan near a beach where they once caught a cold. Once the links are established, people relax in each other's company. Without them, they don't know where to begin. It's partly because the Irish have always been travellers, whose links to home are preserved in stories about where they came from. But it's also because most people living in the Irish countryside can trace their families back for generations; and, like me, almost everyone in Irish cities is only a few generations away from their country roots.

When I first came to Corca Dhuibhne my time was spent walking the roads. Then, they led between fields and up to mountains whose names I didn't know. Now, slowly, as time passes, I'm learning. Walking up from the village with the music of a session lost behind me on the wind, I recognise the fields on either side of me. I need no torch to guide me. The strip of grass that's broken through the road's tarred surface marks its centre; I can feel rough tufts, starred with speedwell and creamy brown-tipped clover, guiding my feet. I know whose sheep are bleating on my right side, and what cows are grazing on my left. I climb the tarred road towards the Clasach, and above and below me in the dusk are smaller roads, untarred and sheltered by high hedges, leading to bogland and to fields. I'm learning their names.

Everyone who was born here knows the relationships between one family and another – who married whom; what land was bought with whose dowry; who inherited which field, and from whom. Names matter, but almost more important is how names are linked to places. People are identified by the house they were born in and the place they married into. Detail's important. And the details reach back across generations, identifying each family with the land that nourished it, and drawing each individual into the web of the community. Families know the sites of houses their families were evicted from in the bad times, when landlords had the power to throw them out on the roads. They know the names of the ships that took people to England and America; of the mines where they worked and died in Canada and Butte, Montana; and of the gangers who gave out jobs to men who carried their shovels to Kilburn and Camden Town.

Even the origins of place names themselves are remembered. Often they've been handed down across millennia. In ancient Ireland, stories that explain place names were given a category of their own, called *dinnseanchas*. If you climb the hill from Ballyferriter village today, or sit looking at the ocean from Síle Gorman's guesthouse, you'll see two rocky headlands that curve round Smerwick Harbour. To the east, at the end of the headland, is an island called *An Charraigh Dhubh*. Its name means 'The Black Rock', which is pretty self-explanatory. To the west is a high peak called *Binn Diarmada*, which means 'Diarmaid's Peak'. Its name's explained in dinnseanchas.

When Fionn Mac Cumhaill married a wife she was the means of resolving a quarrel. Her father, the High King, had quarrelled with Fionn and it was to resolve that quarrel that they arranged the marriage. So that was how Gráinne came to Fionn, as a cow brought from one man's herd to another. Though she made no complaint when the match was made for her.

But when Gráinne came into Fionn's house, she laid her two eyes on the hero Diarmaid Ua Duibhne. Diarmaid's a man from the west, you can tell from his name that his ancestral territory is Corca Dhuibhne. He was as dark as Fionn was fair. His skin was white as lime and his strength was the strength of an oak tree. And Gráinne took a fancy to him.

She sat in the sun bower that Fionn had prepared for her. And her maidservants dressed her, and painted her hands and her feet. They braided her hair, and tied in amber beads, and joined each braid to the next braid with nine threads of silk. Then they brought a silk mantle, embroidered with gold, and fringed with the feathers of cuckoos. It was a gift from Fionn. But Gráinne put it aside and didn't wear it.

That night Diarmaid Ua Duibhne sat next to Fionn at the high table. They were easy together, trusted and trusting, ready to laugh at each other by the campfire and kill for each other in the field. But Gráinne took a golden cup that held drink for nine times nine men. And she added certain herbs to it, such as women use for enchantment. Then she sent her maid to carry the cup round to the whole company. 'Take it to Fionn and to all his companions,' she said, 'but pass by Diarmaid Ua Duibhne.' So the maid did as Gráinne told her. And all who drank from the cup fell into a sleep.

Then Gráinne stood up in the hall, and she spoke to Diarmaid Ua Duibhne. 'Will you take my love, Diarmaid Ua Duibhne, and will you take me out of this house tonight?' 'I will not,' said Diarmaid, 'I will not meddle with the woman that is promised to Fionn.' 'If the silken thread of love will not bind you,' she said, 'I will bind myself to your protection.' This is serious, because, as a member of Fionn's band, he's now honour-bound to take care of her.

Two others in the hall are awake, because they've refused the drugged cup. Oisín, Fionn's son, and Caoilte, a druid. Diarmaid asks their advice and they tell him he's in a no-win situation; his honour's compromised whatever he does. So he turns back to Gráinne and makes his choice. 'It is a bad binding,' said Diarmaid, 'and it is in my mind that it will bring me death. But, since you lay it on me, I must take you,' he said, 'though no good will come of it.'

So Diarmaid takes Gráinne out of the house while Fionn and the rest of the wedding guests are sleeping. And they travel the length and breadth of Ireland, pursued by Fionn, who's driven mad by jealousy. There's no refuge. Wherever they go Fionn's behind them, so Diarmaid makes a bed for himself and Gráinne in a different place each night, all as inaccessible as possible. All over Ireland people still point them out. At one point Diarmaid takes Gráinne to Corca Dhuibhne, because it's the territory of his ancestors, and makes their bed on a peak here, surrounded on three sides by the ocean. He spends the night on guard there, high above the Atlantic. The waves roll below him and the night breathes around him as he sits waiting for Fionn, while Gráinne lies sleeping in darkness. And that's why, according to the story, the peak at the western end of Smerwick Harbour's been known ever since as Binn Diarmada.

I remember reading that story when I was about ten and suddenly realising it's a mirror image of the English story about Lancelot, Guinevere and King Arthur. I could see it was a slightly distorted mirror, skewed by the fact that the two stories came from different times and were rooted in different places. But what they both basically come down to is 'My Best Friend Stole My Wife'. It was another eureka moment, like the realisation I had later about Granny's Too-ha-Day, one of the things in my life that have made me a writer now. I still remember the sense of wonder it gave me. It wasn't just that I'd realised how stories migrate from one place to another, taking on new identities and finding new roots. I'd taken the first step to uncovering what stories are for: they're endless explorations of human nature, in endless attempts to uncover who we are, and what we're doing here.

Years later I recognised the links between fair-haired Fionn's struggle with dark-haired Diarmaid and the ancient story of Lugh, the sun-god striding up Mount Brandon to defeat 'dark, crooked' Crom Dubh. What I love now about Irish storytelling are those echoes and layers of meaning. Stories rooted in visions of gods are also explorations of human life, rooted in the unsentimentality of the countryside. Diarmaid and Gráinne aren't eternality young, star-crossed lovers who die in each other's arms. Instead they get older and tire of the chase. Mutual friends help them to make their peace with Fionn, and they build a house and settle down. Then, years later, when Diarmaid's injured out hunting, Fionn wants to help him, but he can't. All the old hatred and jealousy come back, and he lets Diarmaid die. Gráinne's devastated and swears she'll raise Diarmaid's children to avenge him. But other things intervene, so that doesn't happen either. Instead, as time passes, old passions fade. And in the end, giving her someone to be and her children a place to belong to, she marries Fionn.

In the months when Wilf was working on Tí Neillí Mhuiris, his days were shaped by the coming and going of Jack's cows. Jack had eleven cows then, all born on the farm. They belonged to this place, bred from stock that was here before Jack's family came to this village. In the mornings they knew the way to their pasture, down stony lanes studded with rough grass, green watercress and wild-flowers. In the evenings they'd plod heavily down the road to the cowshed, eager to be milked. They were wide-eyed and timid, uncertain of strangers. Long streams of saliva swung from their jaws and their hair was curled and creamy white, on foreheads a hand span wide. When they passed on the road they'd stop outside our garden, lowering their heads to the stream that runs by the hedge. And Jack would stop for a chat. In Irish the word for 'cow' is *bó*. It's the root of the word *bóthar*, which means 'road' and comes from a time when roads were just ways walked by cows. And the word for a lane in Irish is *bóthairín*, which means 'little road'. Each day, with the dogs running beside them, Jack's cows would turn off the tarred road and head down a bóthairín to the fields. Sometimes they grazed looking over the ocean. Sometimes they'd walk the bóthairín above Tí Neillí Mhuiris and climb to the steep grazing round the tumbled Iron Age walls on the side of the mountain. It's called Cathar na gCat.

The ruin in that field is ancient. But its name comes from a later time, when there were other houses there as well, and other people living there. Whatever those later houses were made of, there's no trace of them now. Like hundreds of the mud and stone cabins that were built here well into the twentieth century, they've disappeared back into the earth. But the story survives.

There was a man who lived in that place once, and he had cats. One was a big cat, with a long tail and a big head on him. He'd fight any rat. He'd hunt him out of the house with a swipe of his big paw that had five sharp nails in it, like five spikes on a rake. And he was a clever cat, with good Irish. One day, when the man was going into town, the cat turned round and looked at him. '*Tóg leat féirín dom ón Daingean,*' he said. 'Bring me a present back from Dingle.' After that people said that the cats in that place were cleverer than their master, and that the place belonged to them and not the man. Cathar na gCat means 'The Fort Of The Cats'. And that's how it got its name.

That story's a folktale. Myths about gods, dinnseanchas about ancient place names like Binn Diarmada and imramma about ancient voyages belong to the older, 'higher' tradition of Irish storytelling. Folktales, which include fairy stories, belong to the 'lower', later one. I remember sitting at Mrs Hurley's window once, writing out lists of stories before an exam, and marking the different groups with coloured highlighters. Green for dinnseanchas (earth), blue for imramma (sea). Then the metaphor ran out and, to this day, I'm stuck with the image that folktales are pink (Barbie). Later I learnt that stories from a living tradition don't all fit neatly into categories anyway. Sometimes they flow and grow and morph into each other. Gods diminish into fairies. And dinnseanchas stories about kings and warriors are echoed thousands of years later in folktales about talking cats. Or green cows.

When you climb the road from Ballyferriter to the Clasach, there's a field on your left called 'the field of the *Glas Gaibhneach*'. In Irish glas means 'green', and you pronounce the name something like Gloss Gy-nock. There's a story about how that field got its name. It goes like this.

There was once a cow in the village of Márthain, and her name was the Glas Gaibhneach. They say she came out of the sea at the beach they call the White Mouth. She was green in colour, and she was a great milker. She was a handsome cow and she'd go from village to village. She'd give milk to anyone who'd milk her, and she'd fill up the vessel to the top. There was a poor, old woman in Márthain at the time, and the Glas Gaibhneach would come to her every morning to be milked. She'd milk the cow into a vessel till it overflowed. A beggar man passed early one morning. 'That's a wonderful cow,' he said, 'but I bet she wouldn't fill the vessel I've got.' 'I bet she would,' said the old woman. The beggar man took out a sieve, and he milked the cow into it. And as the sieve filled up it emptied out again. When the cow saw the milk being wasted, she turned her head and spoke. 'Spare the milk.' The beggar man ignored her, and kept milking till midday. 'Spare the milk,' said the cow again. The old woman was ashamed, but she didn't want to give in and lose her bet. 'Spare the milk,' said the cow the third time. But the beggar man kept on milking. With that, the Glas Gaibhneach started kicking and she gave the beggar man a whack of her hoof. She hit him in the head and he fell dead on the ground. The Glas Gaibhneach went off down to the sea, and no one's seen her since that time. That field is named after her. And my neighbours' cattle graze it now.

Cows have always been important in Ireland. For thousands of years, material wealth here was measured in terms of cattle, and tribesmen carried off their enemies' herds in daring raids called *táin*. One of the oldest stories recorded in Irish is called the *Táin Bó Cuailgne* which means 'the Cattle Raid of Cooley'. It starts with Medb, queen of Connacht, chatting at home in bed with her husband, Aillil. The pillow talk gets competitive when Aillil claims he's wealthier than she is and, basically, has more stuff. So they list their possessions and come out equal. Until Aillil mentions a white bull in his herd which is bigger and stronger than any bull Medb has in hers. Medb's furious, and sends messengers to the king of Ulster asking for the brown bull of Cuailgne, the king's prize bull, which is bigger still. In return she offers him gifts, including 'my own friendly thighs'. Unsurprisingly, the king agrees, but then Medb's messengers get drunk and boast that they'd have taken the bull anyway, if it hadn't been given. So they're thrown out and sent away with nothing.

And that begins the *Táin Bó Cuailgne*, the great 'Cattle Raid of Cooley', when Medb leads the Connachtmen into Ulster to steal the king's brown bull. It's an epic story, and the stakes are raised by the fact that the Ulstermen are all in bed with labour pains, the result of a curse laid on them by a pregnant woman whom the king once forced to run a race with his horse. She cursed them as she went into labour, after beating the horse by a whisker. 'Each man of Ulster that hears my screams,' she screamed, 'will suffer my pains himself, for nine days and nine nights at the time of his greatest danger.'

In some versions of the story she's a goddess, but, anyway, the curse sticks. So, as Medb and the Connachtmen ride into Ulster, the king's warriors are all lying in bed, screaming. And, presumably, wishing they hadn't bet on the horse. The only one not affected by the curse is the teenage Iron-Age hero, Cú Chulainn. And the story ends, after terrible slaughter, with the brown bull killing the white one. Then it goes on a rampage across Ireland, hurling bits of the white bull in all directions and providing the Táin storyteller with opportunities to explain place names. Like the town of Athlone, *Áth Lúan*, which he says comes from the name of a ford where the brown bull tossed the poor white bull's loins. And *Áth Cliath*, the Irish name for Dublin, which is said to mean 'the ford of the ribs'. There's 'the ford of the liver' and 'the port of the hind leg' too. And others, but you get the idea.

Stories about Cú Chulainn have travelled many roads since they were first heard by Iron Age firesides. His adventures were first written down in Ireland in the eleventh century, and since then they've spread all over the world. Now he's a character in Manga-style books and American comics. As I'm writing this, the Táin's being developed as a film in England. And, in the Japanese video games series *Shin Megami Tensei,* Cú Chulainn fights warriors and enchanters, and a bird-headed witch called the Morrigu. In the original story, the Morrigu's one of three sister goddesses who scavenge the battlefield in the form of ravens. They're the dark side of the Good Goddess, three cruel hags without the fertile maiden and the fruitful mother to balance fear of death with hope of rebirth.

At the end of the Táin, a queen's greed annihilates her own army. In the story about the Glas Gaibhneach, greed and pride lead to violent death too. But it's a folktale, so the beggar man dies from the kick of a cow's hoof. It's not heroes' blood that's spilt, it's milk, so it ends with a poor old woman left without food. But both stories carry the same message. Each reflects the lives and the imaginations of the communities that created them. They're explorations of shared human nature, set in recognisable contexts. And in Corca Dhuibhne today, they're still being used for the same purpose.

Stories have always travelled. In the past, pedlars, who sold bundles of goods from house to house, and tinkers, who'd travel from place to place mending pots and trading horses, were given seats by the fire here, and urged to share the stories they'd heard on the road. And local storytellers from different villages would compete against each other, capping one story with another. It was their neighbours who decided which was best.

When I was here as a student, weeks of storytelling like those were still happening. But I wasn't brave enough then to ask if I could come and listen. It always seemed to me that, with an outsider present, the evening would be different, and somehow spoilt. So I remember sitting in a booth in the university in Dublin, listening to recordings of storytellers instead. Some were country tales, full of twists and broad humour. Others were about heroic feats in ancient wars, full of violent passions and stories within stories. The soft, musical voices would suddenly rise in pitch, or drop suddenly, before a dramatic pause. Or they'd slide into formal, melodious runs of words, all starting with the same sound, and poured out on a single breath, like tongue-twisters. The tapes I'd taken from the library were labelled, so I knew the voices came from Corca Dhuibhne. That was why I'd chosen them. But listening in a stuffy booth, facing a blank wall, I couldn't locate them in this vibrant, shining place I'd come to love. Looking back now, I think it was because I was hearing them out of context, and because the familiar audience of neighbours they were used to hadn't been there during the recordings. Sometimes the voices would tail off and then start again, sounding uncertain and muffled. I know now that, faced by microphones held by city scholars, some of the older storytellers I listened to were shy, and unsure of what was wanted. To have captured even a taste of their art on tape was extraordinary.

As with music, certain families here are known for *seanchas*, the art of traditional Irish-language storytelling, passed down through generations. Cáit Feiritéar, who's always called 'Bab', was born in Dún Chaoin in 1916. Mícheál Ó Guithín, her grandfather, and Tadhg Ó Guithín, her uncle, were famous storytellers, who lived in the house where she grew up. And Bab could remember running up to her great-aunt Máire's house as a child. 'She was a woman who loved life. I can see her still, sitting there by the fire with a spinning wheel, and she spinning. She had short, funny stories, and she had long stories too. You couldn't help being interested in them.' Bab listened, and remembered, and became a famous story-teller herself. She was a gentle, reserved woman, with a straight back and a warm sense of humour. When Wilf and I first came to Tí Neillí Mhuiris she was still living in the house she'd grown up in. And, at eighty-five, she was still telling stories.

The nights of epic tales that lasted a week are gone. So are the nights when neighbours gathered in each other's houses each evening, and every house on the peninsula kept an open door. At the end of her life, Bab did much of her storytelling in schools. She recorded stories for researchers and for local radio, and made CDs to go with children's books. She was determined to pass on her store to another generation, now that most kids don't run into their granny or auntie anymore, to hear them told by the fire. Bab was among the last of her own generation; the older people say her storytelling was richer and more complex than anything that's heard now. But the tradition's still seen as precious.

Seanchas is still a competitive art here, with prizes for the best style and the ability to deliver the traditional long, crafted sentences and repeated sound patterns. Last winter, Wilf and I went to a fundraiser for a local hospital, held in a theatre in Dingle. There was a full house and a comfortable sense in the audience that we'd braved the cold weather to enjoy ourselves in a good cause. There were dancers, a gospel choir, a classical quartet and schoolkids in Santa hats, singing carols. People whooped and laughed and parents held up phones to record their kids' first efforts in front of an audience. And topping the bill was a local man who's a prize-winning storyteller.

He sat on a chair in front of a microphone, with his hands planted on his knees, and held the whole house spellbound with a folktale. It was delivered with the same poetic runs, twists and cliffhangers that I'd heard in the stuffy booth in my language lab, facing a blank wall. If I'd been less shy when I first came here, I might have heard his father, or grandfather, telling the same story by a winter fire.

There was a man in this village who told stories in Jack's house when Jack and his sisters were children. His name was Maras Seán Connor, and he'd learnt his stories from his father and grandfather. He told them here in Neillí's house as well. Some were folktales. Others were epic myths and legends, about warrior heroes like Fionn Mac Cumhaill, whose best friend stole his wife, or about Cú Chulainn, who rode with the heads of his enemies dripping blood at the rim of his chariot. Jack can remember them lasting for a week of long winter evenings, each ending with a dramatic cliffhanger and a crowd of neighbours longing for the next instalment the following night.

Like many of their generation, Jack's brother and his three sisters had to leave their home here in Corca Dhuibhne, to find work. They found it in Dublin, where his sister Nóirín met and married a man called Leon

Rowsome. The first time Wilf and I met Nóirín she was home on the farm, on a visit from Dublin. We leant against the wall at the open door, where the hens were pecking mash out of an old frying pan. We talked about the garden, and about a musician we'd heard playing in the village. And Nóirín told us the story of the Rowsome family. It reaches back along many roads, across seven generations.

Nóirín's husband Leon's great-grandfather, Samuel Rowsome, was an uilleann piper and pipemaker in a place in Wexford, called Scarawalsh. Uilleann pipes are a traditional Irish instrument, smaller and quieter than the Scottish bagpipes, with a bag that's inflated by a bellows pumped by the player's elbow. Which is where the name comes from – the Irish for 'elbow' is *uilleann*. Samuel Rowsome's son, William, left home at the end of the nineteenth century, and set up a pipemaking workshop in Dublin. He'd inherited his father's skills in playing, making and repairing pipes, and passed them on to his own son, Leo. Leo, in turn, passed them on to his son, Leon. Who became Nóirín's husband. Leaning against the farmhouse wall, I listened to the list of names and placenames. And I heard myself doing what people in Ireland always do. 'My mother had cousins in Scarawalsh,' I said. 'She was an O'Connor from Enniscorthy, up near The Duffry Gate. Her mother's people were Keoghs.' For the next ten minutes, as the hens fussed round the frying pan, we stood there, naming names and place names. Then, as we left to dig spuds for our dinner, Nóirín stepped into the house and came out with a present of her son Kevin's newly-released CD. He's a piper too.

As Wilf and I walked back up the hill that day, I realised how little I know about where I come from. My own family memories hardly reach back beyond a single generation. I've no idea what land my mother's cousins farmed in Scarawalsh, or where my father's people lived in Connemara. The instinct to name names and make links is still alive in me, but the web of shared memories that shaped my own identity has been broken. The longer I live here in Corca Dhuibhne, the more I understand what I've lost.

Later that year we met Nóirín's daughter Mary, who plays the flute, and Mark, Mary's husband, who plays bouzouki and guitar. Being a Rowsome, Mary's roots are in traditional music, and she and Mark often play at sessions together. But he's just as happy with blues and rock. It was Mark who spotted that Wilf, despite a lifetime working with professional musicians as an opera director, was still too shy to play in a session. By then he'd graduated from playing for the cows in the field behind Tí Neillí Mhuiris, he'd been to the spring music school, and he was happy enough to play at Máire Begley's or here in the house when the neighbours dropped in. But joining in at a pub session was something different. It wasn't part of his culture, and the thought of it freaked him. I suppose I should have noticed, but I didn't. And if I had, not being a musician, I don't know what I could have done about it. But it seemed to take no time for Mark to identify the problem, and, next thing we knew, he'd stepped in and taken a hand.

It all happened so fast there wasn't time to argue. Or even to think. Ballyferriter's the place to find a pub. There are three there, called Tigh Uí Mhurchú, Tigh an tSaorsaigh and Tigh Uí Chatháin – or, in English, Murphy's, Sayers's and Kane's. There's also a bar in the hotel. Because the hotel was newly-opened then, the bar wasn't likely to be crowded. So that's where Mark decided we should go.

It was late afternoon when we arrived and the bar was empty, except for a few hotel guests. Mark led us to a corner near the fire. The instrument cases were put on the table and the floor, and Mark and Wilf went to the bar. As they came back with the drinks I could see Wilf getting increasingly nervous. Mark and Mary's youngest son was with us. He's called Mark Óg, which means 'Young Mark'. Mary and Mark sipped their drinks, took out the flute and guitar, chatted a bit, and began to play. Mark Óg settled into the corner with an orange juice and his PlayStation. Wilf took out the concertina and put it on the table. Then he sipped his coffee. Then he looked over Mark Óg's shoulder. Mark Óg, who has two older brothers, wasn't about to let anyone move in on his PlayStation. He hunched his shoulder and turned away. The concertina stayed where it was on the table and Wilf went back to his coffee.

I don't remember exactly what Mark and Mary played, but they were traditional toe-tapping tunes in the West Kerry style, three tunes played three times each, with the transition from one to the next indicated by a flicker of eye contact between the players. I know that afterwards the tunes were named, and there was discussion about where they came from. Then Mark sang a song. He's a real guitarist, with an assured, elegant style, and the hotel guests turned round at their table to listen. When he finished he nodded at Wilf and said, 'Play a slow air.' I waited to see what would happen, but it was an easy way in. Slow airs are often the tunes of sean-nós songs, quiet and lyrical, and very sweet on the concertina. According to Wilf, his hands were sweating so much his fingers would have slipped off the buttons if he'd tried a reel or a polka. But he started a plaintive lament, and after the first verse, Mary joined in on the flute. Then Mark touched in chords and decoration, all three started to respond to each other's playing, and I watched Wilf relax into the music. When they finished, there was a scatter of applause from the barman and the hotel guests, and Mark Óg took his eyes off his PlayStation for a second and politely announced, 'That was good.' Wilf was still sweating, but Mark and Mary went straight into some polkas he'd played with them back at the house, and he joined in. One tune followed another, and even the arrival of other, unknown, musicians didn't throw him.

For Wilf, that day was a major breakthrough, the start of a process that's given him his own identity here, as a musician. When we got up to go, he tried to thank Mary and Mark. Mark shrugged, 'You just had to break the back of it. You'll be fine now.' For him, it was just a matter of giving encouragement when it was needed, part of an inherited culture they've passed on to their own kids.

Kids here are used to the idea that everyone contributes to a night's entertainment. If your name's called out, you get up and get on with it, without a fuss. And there's no pressure to be brilliant, it's just a matter of sharing your store. There's another proverb that people use here, *mol an óige agus tiocfaidh sí*. It means 'praise youth and it'll come along'. One night Wilf and I were at a party when the chat had drifted into songs, and a freckled six-year-old boy got up to say a poem. He'd been longing to be called on, but halfway through he lost the words. With his hands thrust into the pockets of his Spiderman trousers, he stood there in the centre of the room, slowly going scarlet under his freckles. I looked at his mum, longing for her to step in and rescue him; everything in me wanted to save him from the embarrassment of standing there at a loss. But no one moved. Instead, there was a chorus of support. 'Keep at it, boy, you're doing grand!' 'You have it, don't give up!' His face crumpled, and the encouragement got louder. 'Hold your ground, boy! Start again and give it another go!' With his eyes on his family, who were willing him on, he took a deep breath. This time he got one verse farther on and blanked again. It was clear that he wasn't going to recover, so everyone clapped, and he ran to his mum. As he climbed on her knee, the elderly man beside her smiled down at him, still clapping. 'Fair play to you, boy, you stuck with it. You'll have the whole of it for us next time.' There was no sense of failure, or of pressure to succeed. Just the certainty that everyone there was behind him, and that there'd be another chance to make a name for himself.

Here in Corca Dhuibhne, traditions like those have been preserved because life changed slowly. Jack's sisters can remember their mother's shawl hanging on the back of the door, to be thrown over her head when she went to follow the cows. They can tell you how many turkeys she reared to save money to build the new kitchen. And they tell stories of women who walked to Dingle for supplies carrying their shoes till they reached the outskirts of town, to save shoe leather. People here were poor, but it wasn't just that. It took time for new customs and fashions to arrive, and when they got here people didn't always want them. Mike George says he looked forward to the summers in his childhood, when children ran barefoot to school. 'We couldn't wait to get rid of the shoes. There was freedom without them.' One person's hardship is another person's freedom. In the end it comes down to values, and to what we're taught to expect.

It's also a matter of balance. No one here would want to go back to a time when poverty controlled virtually every aspect of life. It was poverty and lack of opportunity that drove young people out of Corca Dhuibhne and into the cities; just as, in previous generations, poverty and famine had killed hundreds of thousands of their ancestors, and driven whole families overseas. And the same grinding poverty brought harshness into the place they left behind. People here remember brutal schoolteachers, and fear of the priests, and a time when men, in particular, were expected not to show emotion. Some young people were crushed by hard work and lack of choice, and many had to give up their own ambitions to support siblings or ageing parents. Repression and reticence existed alongside encouragement and love. Those memories struck deep, so people reared here shake their heads at recession and debt. They look at a younger generation, used to the days of generous state benefits and endlessly available credit, and worry about how they'll cope. They fear that another generation will have to move from this place to the cities to find jobs. But mostly they square their shoulders and get on with living. 'We know how to weather the bad times,' they say. 'We can do it again.'

And, living here, I'm aware of a balance that's been found between the harshness that was imposed on the people, and the resilience that's part of their inheritance. Looking back now at that freckled kid at the party in his Spiderman trousers, I know my reaction was wrong. It seemed to me that the important thing was to save him from embarrassment. I wanted to protect him, and, I suppose, to protect myself from the sight of his distress. The people here wanted him to grow strong.

Mary Rowsome was brought up in Dublin, and she and Mark live there today. But her roots in this place go deep. She remembers being here as a child, when the men would go down to the village, and she and her granny would sing and play the harmonica. She remembers elderly neighbours who'd welcome her in with bread and jam. And playing with her cousins and siblings in the stream, where Jack made boats for them out of twigs and leaves, and floated them under the bridge. She remembers summers helping on the farm, feeding the hens and following the cows; and getting letters in Dublin from her granny, describing the weather here, and the round of the seasons. She showed me the letters once, carefully preserved in a folder. They're written in blue ink on little sheets of notepaper. '. . . all our early sprouters are turned by frost so we won't have any early spuds this year.'

'. . . Jack is busy setting the mangols . . . we have ten cows calfed now, so it's no rest.' They're quiet echoes of a life of hard work and little money. And they're written in English, the language her children had needed to learn if they were to work in the city. But she signed them in Irish, '. . . *le grá agus gean* . . . with love . . .' And each letter ends with encouragement and praise '. . . I'm so proud of you, dear, and of all of you . . .' Mary's eyes fill with tears when she reads them.

Mary's boys visit the farm now, and hang out here with their cousins. They chase the hens and play with the dogs, and Jack makes them boats of sticks and leaves to sail under the bridge. The kids are learning music, and to speak Irish. Mary's son Seán plays guitar, like his dad, as well as the flute and the mandolin. And Mark Óg, Michael, and their cousin Luke are the sixth generation descended from Samuel Rowsome to play the pipes. Mary's cousin Terry was born in Dublin, but he came back to his roots and his kids are growing up here. Her cousin Catherine was born in Dublin too; now she's married to a man who farms at the foot of Binn Diarmada. At school her kids are learning to tell Bab Feiritéar's story of the Glas Gaibhneach, and to name the names of the fields around their home.

I remember sitting in Jack's kitchen once, listening to his sisters talking about their childhood. 'I loved taking the cows up to the Cathar na gCat', one said. 'I was never happier than to be walking with them on my own.' I asked if she'd been lonely among the crowds in Dublin. 'I was, of course, at first, but, sure we had to go.' Her sisters nodded. 'In those days there was no choice.' Choice has made all the difference. Now, like so many families here with the same story, they, their children, and their children's children keep finding the road back.

10

Enough is Plenty

There's a building in London called the Shard of Glass. As I'm writing this it's still being built. I love it. There are webcams on the building site and I keep sneaking online to watch it rising like a spear from the south bank of the Thames. Around its feet are sooty Victorian streets and blackened railway arches. When it's finished it'll soar staggeringly high into the air above them, clad in glass and finishing in a jagged peak. Already its glass sides are reflecting misty grey light from the London skies. But when I first passed its site it hadn't even broken ground. It was four or five years after we'd found Tí Neillí Mhuiris. I was walking out of London Bridge station to meet Wilf, who'd flown over from Ireland. And I was in a panic about what was going to happen next.

In our first years in Tí Neillí Mhuiris we didn't know how much time we'd be able to spend here. We still don't: it's an organic thing, determined by life and work. But we discovered that an early flight got us to central London in time for morning meetings and, as long as I had an internet connection, I could write scripts just as well here as in London. So our time spent in Tí Neillí Mhuiris increased every year. The problem was that Wilf's time here was beginning to be spent studying how to arrange and compose music. Which meant hours playing the keyboard as well as the concertina. I'm oblivious to most things when I'm working. But it's not easy to write dialogue when someone's repeating particular phrases or rhythms over and over again at the opposite end of the room.

I remember one day when I was dramatising a classic French novel and he was obsessively playing a jig. It all started fairly politely. 'Could you give it a break, Wilf, I'm kind of at an iffy bit.' Silence for about ten minutes while he tapped notes into his laptop. Then the jig started again. I decided that all I needed was focus. So I focused, and I thought I was coping fine. Then, suddenly, I heard myself shouting 'Will you stop playing

JIGS! Everyone I write's started to talk in an Irish accent!'
There was a pause. Then he started to play a hornpipe
called 'Bonaparte's Defeat'. Which practically led to
blows. So we decided we needed another room.

The oldest houses here are long and low, with new
rooms or sheds built out from the old gable ends. So
Wilf designed a new room against our north gable, lower
than the original house and with the same small windows.
When we'd been through the application process and got
our planning permission, we knocked down the old shed
at the end of the house. Billy and one of his sons came
back to build the shell of the new room. We'd decided
to make a kitchen with room for a table to eat at, as well
as a space for Wilf to work in. Mike George's son plumbed
in the water. The angle of the gateway to the road had
to be changed, and Terry, with Cliodhna's dad, who's a
stonemason, took time out to build us new gateposts,
using field stones. The rest was down to Wilf and me.

Looking back now, I know it was too much work. We'd
hardly had time to recover from the first lot, and here
we were again, plastering and painting, putting down a
stone floor, and insulating and putting up a ceiling. The
ceiling took five coats of paint – one of aluminium primer,
two of white undercoat, and two creamy topcoats – to
produce the effect of the thick layers of paint in the other
room. It nearly broke my back.

It had its interesting moments, though. One day, when

Wilf was here on his own putting up the boards, he discovered the reason for the series of inexplicable dents he and Christy Corduff had noticed in the other room. He was working his way across the new room, off ladders. As he reached the centre, the length of the boards began to make it impossible for him to hold them in place while nailing them up. So he decided to prop the far end of the board he was working on with an upright board, braced against the floor. It took a couple of tries to get the prop wedged against the ceiling board. But it worked. When the board was nailed up he removed the prop. Then he looked up to check the work. And there in the board he'd just nailed up was exactly the same series of dents that he and Christy had wondered at in the ceiling of the other room. A hundred years earlier, when Neillí's house was being built, one man working on his own had hit exactly the same problem Wilf hit. And found exactly the same solution.

So there were interesting bits, but it was hard, relentless slog. I painted most of the ceiling off a heavy scaffold in the middle of the room. It was a beast to move and to work from, but not as bad as the time I spent teetering on ladders to reach the highest points of the room at either end. I don't like ladders. Wilf cut and laid stone, fitted windowsills, wired in lighting, built bookshelves, cupboards and a new kitchen. I finished painting the ceiling and started painting everything else. Wilf turned the tiny 1970s extension into a utility room. We carried the oven and the fridge through to the new kitchen and installed them. We didn't want the new room to pretend to be an old one, but we were determined it wouldn't look or feel like something tacked on to the rest of the house. So everything was handmade and finished with the same care as before. The stone floor sloped gently towards the old room with the lie of the land. The doorway between the two rooms was cut through the two foot thick wall on one side of the fireplace. Billy found a door for it in his shed, solid enough to deaden the sound of 'Bonaparte's Defeat'. Among the stones he took from the wall was one with a flat base and a central, circular depression that seemed to have been worked by a tool; at some time in the past it had stood by the hearth in some other, older house, where pots hung over the fire from an iron crane. Over the years, the turning foot of the crane had worn a perfect circle into the stone. That other house sheltered a family in its time. Then its walls and the hearth they enclosed must have fallen back into the earth. I don't know how long ago that was. But I know that nearly a hundred years ago someone building Neillí's walls reached for a stone and found that one to hand.

When the room was done it was another airy, empty space with the new kitchen wrapped around a little cell for Wilf's desk, enclosed by painted six-foot walls like screens. The ceiling was deep cream, the other timber was painted shades of grey, and, like the old rooms, the walls were rough plaster, painted creamy white.

Outside, we repaired the havoc in the garden caused by digging the foundations and moving the gate, by shifting barrow-loads of earth and heaving stones to edge a new path and rebuild the boundary wall. In bed at night I used to feel as if I was falling, even though I was lying flat on my back. In the mornings I ached all over as if I'd been beaten. Wilf was working longer hours than I was, which wasn't good for him either; as well as the work he was doing in the house, he'd got Terry to help him use the blocks from the demolished shed to repair Paddy's byre in the garden, and then roofed it himself.

It was a new commitment to Tí Neillí Mhuiris. We were sure it was right, because being here was even better than we'd thought it would be. But we still needed a London base. By that time we'd lived in the London house for almost eighteen years. We had good neighbours there. Geoff, a builder who lived down the road, had helped when we were working on the house there. He's an artist as well as a skilled tradesman and over the years we'd become friends. And when Wilf was working here on Tí Neillí Mhuiris Geoff was always there in a crisis, at the end of a phone. 'Hi, Geoff it's Wilf.' 'Hello, mate, how's it going?' 'I've gone blank. What's the mix for exterior render?' 'Four to one, sand and cement.' 'Cheers'.

'No problem, how's the bathroom?' 'Still can't get a fix on that waste pipe.' Long pause. 'Have you tried hitting it?'

There were other friends too, and walks we were used to taking and familiar routines we'd got to know. But we had more space in London than we needed. So, to pay for the new room in Tí Neillí Mhuiris, and the time it was taking to do it, we'd decided to sell the London house and buy a flat. This meant that, while we were building here, we were coping with the added stress of selling, buying and moving from a house to a flat over there.

In showbusiness you get used to working non-stop till something's done. There's no such thing as too much work. When it's there you take it, because you've no idea when, or how, the next job will come. So if several jobs come along at once, or overlap a bit, most people in the business grab them, and put everything else on hold. It's a world in which 'resting' doesn't mean taking a rest. It means coping with unemployment.

The trouble is that, after a lifetime of that approach at work, it's easy to apply it to everything. When you're used to going from an all-night technical rehearsal to a full day of admin followed by long brainstorming sessions with writers and composers, you don't see anything odd in tackling several major projects at once. And when you live in a world in which shows that take years to develop can get dumped in pre-production by email, you get used to thinking you're immune to stress. So, when Wilf and I made our plan we'd just assumed we'd get on with it. We'd be knackered but the job would get done.

At least, that's what was supposed to happen. What I hadn't reckoned on was that, suddenly, I'd go limp. One day, in the midst of everything, my mind and my body just stopped behaving normally. I was exhausted. I couldn't think. At one point, when we were simultaneously working on the new room in Tí Neillí Mhuiris, I was writing to a deadline, and the house in London was under offer, I found myself sitting down on any available surface and sobbing. Wilf stayed focused and tried to regroup. We hadn't yet exchanged contracts in London, did I want to walk away from the sale? I did, with all my heart, but not because I wasn't up for it. I just hadn't the strength for it. But walking away made no sense. We couldn't afford it. And it'd be unfair to the strangers to whom we'd agreed to sell.

We intended to move into the middle of the city, so that when we were in London we could walk to the West End and the concert halls. Wilf had fallen in love with an area on the Southbank, near Tower Bridge. But finding the right place was proving impossible, and adding to the stress. And now I was feeling so wimpy that the area itself began to seem scary. Would a flat there be too noisy? Were the streets safe at night? I'd never worried about walking anywhere in London before. Now I felt I might fall off unfamiliar pavements or get dizzy crossing the road. We were running out of time and options. And all I could do was keep whingeing that I was *tired*.

Looking back now, I can see that was a perfectly accurate expression of my state. I know too that dismissing my reaction as whingeing was actually part of my problem. I was possessed by the idea that I ought to be able to do anything I set my mind to; and that saying it had all got too much was somehow wrong.

The day I walked out of London Bridge station and past the Shard's building site, I was going to meet Wilf to look at flats. He was still working long days on the new room in Ireland and was coming to meet me in London straight from the airport. It was summer and the streets were hot. The estate agent was sweating in his shiny suit, his hair stiff with product and his eyes on his performance targets. Wilf and I sat squashed in the back of his car as he drove us from one unsuitable flat to another, cursing the congestion charge and the colleagues who'd grabbed his secret, personal parking spaces. I could feel tears pricking my eyes as Wilf and I endlessly repeated the same lines. 'No, we're looking for someplace quiet.' 'That floor won't take a piano.' 'We don't want three bathrooms'. And – to the announcement that two of them could easily be converted into bijou studies – 'We're NOT looking for another BUILDING PROJECT.'

It was yet another wasted morning, and as we sat in a

café afterwards, we got a call from the agent who was selling our house. I could see it wasn't good. When Wilf put his phone on the table beside his half-eaten almond croissant he looked as tired as I felt. With two days to exchange of contracts, our purchasers were playing mind games, and the agent was panicking. 'He says if we don't play ball they'll pull out.'

We didn't play ball and the sale went through, but the mind games continued right to the wire. The pressure made me even more panicky. I remember observing with vague interest that I was hyperventilating. And I remember nights lying awake counting down the days to the looming possibility that I'd have to find somewhere to store every-thing from the London house because we couldn't find a flat. But then, suddenly, something went click inside me and I managed to get a grip. One morning, when Wilf had gone back to Ireland to work on the new room, I woke with a new plan. I'd get on a train, go into the centre of London and walk the streets I'd thought were too scary. And I'd behave as if I were walking in Corca Dhuibhne.

I headed for railway arches and deserted lanes between housing estates. I walked past derelict warehouses, beyond the bits of the riverside where the combination of Manhattan-style loft living and the ultra-cool Design Museum had encouraged shiny restaurants and shops. I cut through dusty playgrounds where twisted slides and benches were covered in spray-can graffiti. And whenever I passed someone I looked them straight in the eye and smiled.

Admittedly there were a few nervous reactions and cold stares. But almost everyone smiled back. Kids in hoodies occasionally looked a bit startled. But most of them grinned, and lots said hi. One guy hunkered down beside me and chatted as we admired his Rottweiler. The dog had a gleaming coat, a pink, drippy tongue, and a leather collar studded with fake diamonds. The guy had a matching diamond earring.

In a windy corridor between two high-rise council blocks, I stopped an elderly lady with a shopping bag. I told her my husband wanted us to move into the area and I was scared. What were the buses like? Where would I buy a pint of milk? She was in her seventies, a small, wrinkled woman with wispy hair, dyed bright red and dragged back by a leopard-print slide. I told her how long we'd lived in the house and how leaving suddenly seemed terrifying. We stood there, with old chip papers whipping round our ankles, and she remembered being moved out of the neighbourhood by the council, when her flats were bombed during the war. 'I hated it, love. We were stuck right down the Isle of Dogs and we didn't like it. This was our patch here. All our family lived here. My uncle was over there. My nan was round the corner. And when they moved us we was all separated.' Her eyes were watering in the wind. 'Mind you, it was all right, the place they gave us, but it wasn't the same.'

She took my elbow and led me to the corner of the block. 'See that way through there? There's a market on that side where you get your fish. And a grocers and that. They're nice people.' I asked when she'd come home to her patch. 'They moved us back after the war, when they built the new blocks. Well, everything round here was flattened. It's not like it was, mind, but it's where I was born. And it's your neighbours that matter.' I thanked her and said I was sorry for keeping her standing in the wind. 'That's all right, love, I don't mind. But you don't want to fuss. You'll be fine.'

When we said goodbye she walked off in the direction of the shops. Then she turned and gesticulated, so I followed her. When I caught up with her she leaned towards me, confidentially. 'You want the chippie on the left, mind, I wouldn't trust the other one. Sump oil, that's what my husband says he fries in. Turns his stomach anyway. I reckon it's dodgy lard.'

When I left the lady with the leopard-print slide I took a deep breath and kept walking. I passed the market with the dodgy chippie, and walked through back streets to the Old Kent Road. It was lined with shops selling sacks of rice and boxes of figs, and packets and tins with labels in French and in Arabic. There were piles of watermelons and boxes of salt fish. The cavernous supermarkets sold spit-roasted chickens and smelt of rosewater and spices. I passed little cafés where portly middle-aged men were drinking tiny syrupy cups of coffee. When I went in for a takeaway they glanced at me with the same slightly guarded curiosity I'd seen years ago on farmers' faces in Corca Dhuibhne pubs.

On Tower Bridge Road a queue of women was cheerfully gossiping outside Manze's pie, mash and eels shop. The façades of the buildings were grubby but, ahead of me, the road to the river was lined with tall trees. The sun was filtering through the leaves, dappling the pavement. As I walked on, a thrush swooped from a tree to a hedge. The leaves rustled; the bird's breast was speckled like a creamy, black-tipped clover flower. I walked on down Bermondsey Street, stepping into the road to avoid scaffolding over newly-developed shops. Al's Café, obviously local, was selling egg and chips at Formica-topped tables. Minimalist coffee shops, obviously incomers, were selling organic flapjacks and miso soup. There was a distinct danger that one might morph into the other and become happening retro-chic. But the guy in an apron in Al's doorway chatting with his neighbour from the barber's shop looked pretty rooted. They'd probably seen fashions in retail come and go before.

Outside a church I smelt baking bread; in a window across the road a neon-tube sign said 'Ticino's Bakery, bread baked on the premises twenty-four hours a day'. There was a park crowded with office workers eating lunch on the grass. An unlikely pink and orange building, which was the Fashion and Textile Museum. Then another dark, forbidding tunnel under a railway arch. And then, across a noisy road, huge modern office blocks, like shining cliffs between me and the river. Cutting through them, straight as a die, a paved walk, bisected by an elegant conduit of running water, ran towards slender fountains rising like wellsprings from a stone plaza by the Thames. Executives in suits streamed along either side of the conduit, swinging their designer briefcases. And crouched by the narrow stream of water there were kids sailing paper boats.

We found a flat eventually. Another couple of airy spaces where we could both work, in an old factory building in Bermondsey. With one bathroom, good neighbours and a floor that can take a piano. To the very last minute the move was stressful. Telling myself that moving was my own choice – that no one had dropped bombs on me – helped a bit. But in fact we got through it with help from friends. Showbusiness is a community too, with traditions of mutual support and generosity much older and stronger than gossip columns and celebrity magazines suggest.

When our buyers had viewed the London house the wife went into ecstasies about the garden. She loved that it was organic. She loved the table we'd made from the apple tree when it died; the frog and the rose Wilf's mum had given us; and May's lilies-of-the-valley; and Kath's white flowers, that had spread from the flower bed into the grass. She urged me to leave the herb box we'd under-planted with cyclamen. 'I just love the thought of those little white flowers, waiting to grow.' We'd planned to take that with us, and a bay tree Wilf had brought with him from his own flat when we were married. But the tree had rooted in the garden, and she said she loved it too. The mind games were still going on, via their solicitor. But we'd decided they were probably as stressed out by the process as we were. So we left everything in the garden as it was. I don't miss the house. Other people will live there and be happy. But I grieve for the garden. As soon as the buyers moved in they got a garden designer to chuck the lot in a skip, pave it out and put in a water feature.

I didn't hear about that until much later. When we moved into the new flat I was so tired that I fell into bed and slept for two days. When I got up I got sense. I put the stress of the move behind me, listened to what my body had been telling me, and left most of the unpacking unfinished for months. Then I took myself back here to Corca Dhuibhne. I walked long roads between high flow-ering ditches and watched the changing seasons, and the high clouds reflected in the ocean, and the changing moon, waxing and waning as the world turned from west

to east. I took time to eat and sleep, and taste the vegetables in the garden, and bake my own bread. And, as I'd
hoped when we first came to live here, I brought that
new awareness back to London.

I'm not good at eating eels. But pie and mash shops
selling jellied eels and a green, parsley gravy called 'liquor'
are a London tradition. So as soon as we were settled in
the new flat, Wilf dragged me down the Tower Bridge
Road to Manze's. 'You don't have to eat eels, the pies are
mince.' I wasn't sure I wanted to eat anything where other
people were eating eels. But from the first day I'd passed
Manze's I'd wanted to see inside. So I went along.

It's a beautiful shop, the oldest of its kind still in business today. We passed the queue for takeaways, which
always stretches along the pavement at lunchtime, and
found seats on a narrow, high-backed, wooden bench at
a long, shared table. There were bottles of vinegar and
pepper and salt on the white marble tabletops. The walls
were mirrored, and tiled in cream and green with a
narrow chequered band and cream and brown embossed
edging. Behind the counter, ladies in aprons were slap-
ping dollops of mashed potato onto plates of pie, and
doling out liquor. I don't know what the jellied eels
looked like. I averted my eyes when I saw them being
tipped into soup plates. But, as I watched buckets of mash

hauled up from the basement kitchen in a rattling lift, I realised the atmosphere felt remarkably like a pub in Corca Dhuibhne. This was urban service, though. Speedy and organised, with no time for chat about the weather.

Wilf went to queue at the counter. A large woman and a wide-eyed toddler crowded onto the bench opposite me. A girl in her twenties, obviously the toddler's mum, took a purse out of her bag and joined the queue. The toddler squirmed round in his seat and she looked back reassuringly. 'You stay with Gran, I'm just getting your dinner.' He opened his mouth to roar and then made a sudden sideswipe at a vinegar bottle instead. His gran and I grabbed it simultaneously. Then he sat back angelically, kicking his heels. His gran rolled her eyes and we smiled at each other.

Over her shoulder, bunched together in a corner, I could see a boy and two girls. The boy had a video camera on his shoulder and the girls were festooned in bags and stopwatches. As I watched, one of them edged forward and fluttered apologetically at two men who were eating at a table near the door. She reached between them, moved a mug of tea a fraction, and discreetly backed away. The boy, who was lining up a shot, registered satisfaction. Then my own eyeline was blocked as the toddler's mum slid into her seat.

The grandmother jerked her head at the crew in the corner. 'That's got to be the third this week.' The girl looked round, saw the camera crew, and grinned. 'What are you like? No, it's not.' Her mother raised her voice. 'It is. They're never out of the place.' She spotted a woman at the next table laughing, and winked at her. 'That'll be one of them gritty documentaries. They'll be asking for interviews next. I was in here, last week it was, and this chap came round wanting local colour. Stories of old Bermondsey.' She nodded at her daughter, who grinned back and fed her the next line. 'Go on then, tell us what you said.' The men at the table by the door had turned their heads. Glancing round to make sure of her audience, her mum slapped the table with the flat of her hand. '"Bermondsey?", I said, "don't ask me about Bermondsey! I'm from Walworth!"' There was a happy roar of laughter. Walworth's just across the roundabout, and a mile or so up the road.

In Corca Dhuibhne it's salted ling instead of eels, eaten boiled with onion sauce. But the specific sense of place is identical. And the slow build-up to her punchline was worthy of any pub in Ballyferriter.

The work on the new room in Tí Neillí Mhuiris got done eventually. As I type this, Billy's door between the two rooms is open and I can hear Wilf taking a break from his keyboard to make a sandwich for lunch. The bread traditionally baked here is soda bread, which needs buttermilk. I've always made it when I'm here in Ireland. But for years I didn't make it in London because butter-milk there was dear and hard to find. In Bermondsey we found shops selling bread baked in Ticino's, and markets and delicatessens offering everything from freshly-made croissants to naan. So we had no lack of choice, which is part of the pleasure of being there. But now, since we've been in the new flat, I bake soda bread in both countries. You can get huge cartons of buttermilk down the Old Kent Road.

Looking back, I can hardly remember the exhaustion I felt in the months when the new room was being built. But I know that I did too much and I won't let it happen again. I've recognised too that exhaustion was the expression of a deeper problem. I suppose it was ironic. Ever since I was seventeen I'd been finding my way back to Corca Dhuibhne, where awareness is a central part of life. But, on the way, I'd lost touch with awareness of my own health.

Our bodies are designed to tell us when we've had enough of something. And in a sane world we listen to the message and we stop. But we live in a world in which extremes are good and saying you've had enough is just pathetic. So the more our bodies send us warnings the more we find ways to reject them. If we're tired we reach for wonder supplements to boost our energy. If we're in pain we take extra-fast-acting, ultra-powerful analgesics to suppress our symptoms. We do it because we've bought into the idea that we're morally required to 'challenge' ourselves. So we give ourselves lectures about how we ought to be, instead of listening in silence to see how we are.

When I first came to Corca Dhuibhne I heard a proverb that means 'enough is plenty'. I wrote it down then because of its concise use of Irish and, if I thought about its meaning at all, I assumed it applied to food and drink. Now I think it applies to all the appetites, including our appetite for work and for personal challenge. Too much or too little of anything means lack of balance. The Celts believed that the health of each individual affects the health of the universe. I don't know if that's true. But I do know that the essence of health is balance. And I think the route to finding it is awareness in stillness.

Traditionally, Irish poets composed in darkness. Poems were shaped and preserved in the mind, not in writing. Each was honed in silence, in a dark cell where the poet lay on his back with a heavy stone on his chest. It was a tradition that recognised the importance of silence and stillness. The poems are miracles of tranquil awareness, in which the poet, focusing on single, specific images, reflects on the nature of life.

All over Corca Dhuibhne you find echoes of the people who made those early poems. They were made in solitary places, high on the mountains or out on headlands, by

Christian monks and nuns. You can still find the ruins of their little stone huts, shaped like beehives. The first Christians who came to Ireland brought with them a tradition of prayer in solitude. It had spread across Europe from the Eastern Mediterranean, and when it first got here it fused with the pagan Celtic world view. To the Celts, life on earth was an endless circle. To Christians it's a preparation for eternal life spent in heaven. But, for generations, both pagan Celts and Christian converts climbed Mount Brandon and prayed where blue curves edged with silver burn against the purple dusk. They shared an idea of 'thin places', where awareness of the spirit was heightened by the powerful presence of earth, sea and sky.

But, as time passed, the Church in Rome decided that Irish Christians had moved too close to the pagan world view. Actually, it wasn't as simple as that, things never are. There were politics and local power struggles involved as well. But the official god definitely wasn't supposed to be pulsing through the universe as a balanced, fertile flow of energy. Instead, god was supposed to be male, celibate and living in heaven. So over the centuries reformers turned up in Ireland, like inspectors from Head Office. Edicts went out, bishops and priests got sent on refresher courses, and – officially, at least – 'Celtic Christianity' gradually disappeared. But it must have been good while it lasted. And, unofficially, it never really went away.

On one of my first visits to Mrs Hurley's, I set out to find Gallarus Oratory. I knew it was somewhere on the mountain, part of a ruined monastic site. It's a tiny, boat-shaped, Celtic Christian church. I'd seen a picture of it in a book. Mr Hurley told me how to get to it and I set out on a damp day to climb the narrow roads above Smerwick Harbour. There's a coach park below the oratory now, and loos and a shop, and marked paths leading to a restored enclosure. But on that first day I found it in a high, boggy field with long grass growing round its walls.

It's entirely made of stone. The doorway looks out to the ocean. The curved walls rise to a low ridge, running from front to back, like the keel of an upturned boat. The corner stones of the walls are neatly angled and jointed, narrowing from the base to the smooth line of the roof. The doorway's in the west gable, narrowing from the base to the heavy stone lintel. The threshold's a stone flag. That day, as I waded towards it through wet grass, it seemed dank as a cave. The walls were speckled with grey and yellow lichen. Heavy, grey clouds hung over the mountain. The ocean was a dull, pewter colour and the air I breathed was thick with moisture. For a moment I felt the same feeling I'd felt that first night here, in the darkness on the road. It was night then and now it was broad daylight. But again there seemed to be no edge to anything.

There was just the sky, the ocean, the wet earth and myself.

I stopped on the threshold, in the narrow doorway, between walls that are four foot thick. The floor inside was muddy. Light slanted down from a small, round-topped window high in the opposite gable end. I hesitated, peering into the shadows, smelling damp earth and stone. Then there was a heart-stopping scuffle in a corner, and something low and heavy blundered towards me. I jumped back, feeling my feet skidding on the wet threshold. And a sheep bolted through the doorway, followed by two lambs. I turned as they passed me, and at that moment, with my back to the stone doorway, I saw the mist rise from the ocean. The sun blazed through breaking clouds and the waves between the Black Rock and Binn Diarmada became lines of rippling light.

Inside the oratory the weight of the stone roof and walls seems to hold you fixed against the earth. There's no evidence of an altar. High on the east gable are mounts for a hanging lamp or a book. On the inner face of the doorway the stones are grooved to hold a door frame. When the heavy, timber door was closed the space would have felt smaller still. I don't know if one monk or nun lived in it, or if it was used as a church. But whoever prayed there would have been utterly focused on prayer. And intensely aware, at the same time, of light rippling on the ocean beyond the enclosing walls.

Standing there, I remembered a poem that was written down in Ireland over a thousand years ago. It's about a king called Suibhne who's so freaked by the clamour of war that he goes mad, sprouts wings and flies away from it. The warriors below throw darts and spears at him as he struggles and screams through the air – '. . . pure blue water is good; clean fierce wind is good; green watercress is good . . . I don't like the noise of trumpets; badgers calling in badger-haunted mountains are more musical; I'm tense when horns are blowing . . . a stag's call is a sweeter sound . . .' and he flies on, desperately searching for peace.

Today, at my desk in Tí Neillí Mhuiris, I opened the same book to read the poem again. I chose the lines I've quoted here and I typed them. Then I flipped a few more pages and found this. 'A hedge of trees surrounds me; a blackbird sings songs to me . . . above my lined books the birds' chanting sings to me. A clear-voiced, grey-cloaked cuckoo sings from a fortress of bushes. The Lord is good to me; I write well in a forest of trees.'

In the summer of the year we moved to Bermondsey, Wilf and I took a boat out with friends to the back of the Blasket Islands. Huge colonies of seabirds breed there in isolation. The moving waves were ripples of light and I watched the whirling birds through curtains of spray.

Then Tíaracht, the most westerly island, reared up ahead of us, like a dark tower rising from the crystal ocean. It's an island made of two steep pinnacles of black rock linked by a narrow ridge that forms the top of a massive sea arch. I remember the deep sound of the waves heaving against its towering walls, the high jets of white spray, and the blinding blue light seen through the narrow black tunnel. Shearwaters with beady black eyes swirled past us on up currents of air. Their wings were rigid in flight. Light reflected from the glittering ocean made the sheer, black sides of the island gleam like polished glass. Its jagged peak was black against a silver sky.

Watching the shearwaters, I remembered it was out behind Tíaracht that Maria's Jimmy met a leatherback turtle. He saw it at a distance to begin with, a dark, heavy body moving towards him in a current. At first he thought it was a drowned man. Then, as it came nearer, he saw its blue-black, rubbery back and backswept flippers. No one knows the length of a leatherback turtle's lifespan; as a species they've lived in the oceans over sixty-five million years. This one was hundreds of miles away from his normal feeding ground, presumably swept towards the Blaskets by freak currents. When it reached the fishing boat it set a parallel course to it and swam lazily alongside, its jaws open for jellyfish. When Jimmy told us the story he grinned. 'We were no bother to each other. I didn't want his jellyfish and he didn't want my lobster.

We were both just back there fishing in the sun.' So, happily coexisting in their two different worlds, they kept each other company till the turtle swam away.

Looking back now, I can pinpoint that return to Corca Dhuibhne after we made the move to Bermondsey as the date when my own life tipped farther into balance, and each place brought new awareness of the other. I can see the Shard of Glass now from outside our Bermondsey flat. When I look at its gleaming shape, like a crystal spear rising from a dark sea of buildings, in my mind's eye I see Tíaracht as a dark tower rising from a crystal ocean.

11

Nothing is Unimportant

Animals share the landscape with us; but they know it in ways we don't. Their senses of sight and smell and hearing are different and they can communicate with each other in ways we still don't understand. We hunt them for food. Sometimes we find ways to communicate and cooperate. But, in the end, they're still mysterious. They have secret, complicated lives. In the oldest stories of all, the gods themselves appear as animals. They're wild and powerful, unpredictable and enigmatic. The Good Goddess of plenty is a scavenging bird on the battlefield. A hare brings either a curse or a message from the moon. The myths in which they appear are expressions of fear, hope and possibility in a world where the turning wheel of the seasons offers the promise of rebirth.

To people who've told and retold those stories across millennia, the fact that their edges have often been blurred and their images rewoven doesn't matter. Sometimes the different versions contradict each other, but that in itself is worth remembering. A tradition based on shared memories recognises that nothing is unimportant. It's not a process of selection. Each story that's preserved is valued for the light it sheds on all the others. Because they're all just attempts to make sense of life and death.

It's ten years since Wilf and I came to live here in Tí Neillí Mhuiris. Neighbours we'd smile at on the road or meet in the shops are now our friends. As time's passed and we've been welcomed into the community we've begun to share its rites of passage. We've been invited to weddings, our friends have had babies, kids we know have grown up and gone to college. We've cheered for the local football teams, and baked cakes for birthdays. And we've followed coffins to the burial grounds in Dún Úrlann and Dún Chaoin.

Wilf and I first met Mikeen Sullivan, Maria's dad, one lunchtime in Bric's pub. When we walked into the pub it was cool and shadowy and we passed Mikeen without seeing him. He was sitting at the end of the bar near the door, having a pint with some men. Wilf and I were deep in some unimportant argument. We sat at the far end of the bar, near the kitchen, put in an order for soup and kept talking. Then Mikeen strolled down the bar to say hello. He stopped beside us, leant over, inserted a bony knuckle between Wilf's ribs, and announced that he knew who we were. 'I can tell by the look of you.' I'm not sure what we looked like – probably just cross. But you could tell by the look of him what Mikeen was. He was a horse man.

Mikeen grew up with horses – rode, drove, doctored, bought and sold them. He was a handsome, sunburned man with narrow, gleaming eyes, a hawk's profile and a broad-brimmed hat. Whenever I think of him now, I remember the sound of a horse's hooves on the road, and the sight of a cart swinging round a corner with Mikeen at the reins. I remember him dancing at Maria and Jimmy's wedding, when Maria looked like a slim, white lily as he waltzed her round the floor. And I see him here by the fire in Tí Neillí Mhuiris, grabbing Wilf's hand and singing a song in a voice like a creaky gate. When we met him that first time in Bric's he shook our hands and told us his name. Two sentences later he said he could see that we were fond of each other. 'I was watching you from the other end of the bar, I could tell by the way you were talking to each other.' I laughed and said we'd been fighting like cats. He knuckled Wilf in the ribs again and grinned at us. 'You were, of course. What's that got to do with it?'

When Mikeen was a young man he went to London, to work on the building sites. Then, when other neighbours took the same road, he found work for them too, and places to stay. He made friends in the London Irish community from Camden Town to Hammersmith and Kilburn. Being a horse man, he made contact with English horse dealers. And, while he was in England, he made friends among the Travellers who gather each year, in Cumbria, for the Appleby Horse Fair.

More than ten thousand Gypsies and Travellers, as well as thousands of other visitors, gather in Appleby in June to buy and sell horses. It's the largest fair of its kind in the world and it's been happening for the past three hundred years. The countryside round the little English town becomes crowded with wagons, carts and caravans; there's food and drink and music; and horses are washed in the river before their owners show off their paces, in fields and on the roads. That first day, leaning on the bar at Bric's, Mikeen asked us where we lived in London. Then he asked if we'd been to Appleby Fair. We hadn't, but Wilf had been to the Nottingham Goose Fair; it's older than the fair at Appleby, though now it's more about rollercoasters, water rides, giant wheels and dodgems. But when Wilf mentioned it Mikeen wasn't interested. To him a fair wasn't a fair without horses. And a life without horses was no life at all.

The old people here say one of the greatest changes in Corca Dhuibhne is that horses aren't used anymore on the farms. 'You'd hear them all the time on the roads,' they say, 'and you'd see them working in the fields. Every family here had a horse once, and maybe a couple of donkeys, that pulled carts and carried baskets of turf from the bog.' But now when horses pass on the road they're mostly ridden by tourists.

Mary Rowsome remembers standing in the sunshine when she was on holidays here as a child, waiting for Jack to bring the horse and cart round from the yard. Every second day of the week he'd lift the heavy milk churns into the cart from a concrete plinth by the road. Then the kids would climb in on either side of them, holding onto the handles, and they'd drive the milk to the creamery. The creamery was beside Bric's then, and Bric's had the bar counter on one side and the shop counter on the other. Mary remembers horses and carts tied up outside and the men inside leaning on the bar, discussing the price of milk. If the kids were lucky they'd get a packet of crisps to eat out in the cart, with their legs swinging over the tail.

I remember horses tethered outside pubs and shops myself, in the days when I was staying with Mrs Hurley.

And, in our first years here in Tí Neillí Mhuiris, I remember following the cows to the fields one day with Jack, and hearing about the days when the hay came home piled high on horse-drawn carts. As Jack and I walked the bóthairín that day, there were loose stones under our feet, with mint growing in running water between them. The smell of mint crushed by the cows' hooves filled the narrow tunnel between stone walls that were lost in fuchsia and briars. Flies buzzed round our heads, and the dogs were behind us, splashing between stones. We followed the cows' swaying haunches and Jack talked about the cartloads of hay that once swayed between the same flowering hedges. Back then, when the neighbours would all work together on the harvest, the roads were loud with the sound of horses' hooves. Times have changed. Jack's horse and cart have been replaced by a tractor, and he doesn't milk cows anymore. Yesterday when I walked past the farm I stopped by the concrete plinth in the road where the milk churns used to stand. The dogs lie on it now, and use it as a lookout post.

But there are still donkeys and horses in the fields here, and horse fairs in villages. And local kids, as well as professional jockeys, compete each year at the races on Béal Bán.

Béal Bán's the white curve of beach you can see from the road above Ballyferriter. In English its name means 'white mouth'. It looks out on Smerwick Harbour, the deep, curve of water bounded by Binn Diarmada and the Black Rock. When Mikeen and his generation came home from working in England and America they revived a traditional race day on Béal Bán strand. I remember his eyes gleaming in the shadowy bar in Bric's as he ordered pints, hitched himself up onto a barstool, and told us all about it. What he described was a tradition that stretches back through millennia to when horses themselves were gods.

All over the world people have imagined gods with animal qualities, and seen animals as godlike, or as gods in disguise. Sometimes particular creatures became images of particular gods, or of the goddess; like the fish in Jack's story, that lived in the well across the road from us here in Tí Neilli Mhuiris. At other times specific animals were sacred to individual gods. Horses belonged to Lugh, the Celtic sun-god with flashing eyes and golden hair whose picture I first saw as a child in a book of fairy tales. There was another picture too, which showed him riding across the dawn sky in a chariot pulled by golden horses. Later I read about stories in which Lugh himself is represented as a horse; and in some stories he marries the goddess, who's called The Mother Of Mares. Sitting in Bric's that day with Mikeen, I suddenly remembered reading about houses where as many as forty horses' skulls have been found under the floor. They were sacrifices to the god, buried when the houses were built to ensure his constant presence. And as long as they remained there they acted as echo chambers for dancing feet above them, to remind the god that the people who lived there relied on his protection.

The Béal Bán races are held at the time of the festival of Lughnasa, which takes its name from the god. Lughnasa was the Celts' name for the third season of the year, the months before the harvest. Now it's also the Irish language word for August. It's a season of hard work for farmers and fishermen but it starts with celebration and feasting. Back west, when the tide's out, Béal Bán's long stretch of sand's marked out as a racecourse. Jeeps and tractors arrive pulling horseboxes; bookies set up stands alongside beer and burger stalls; loudspeakers blare out music, and announcements in Irish and English; and the whole neighbourhood drives and walks to the sand dunes, carrying picnics. It's a massive family day out as well as a serious racing event.

Races at Lughnasa belong to an ancient tradition of feasting and horse racing at turning points in the year. They were dedicated to Lugh, whose shining presence gave his people time to save their harvest, and to celebrate his union with the goddess, whose fertility ensured harvests to come. But they also honoured the dead. People believed that as the seasons changed the edges of the fabric of time gave way, allowing powerful forces to seep through. At those shadowy points between one thing and another, the dead returned to mingle with the living and their presence was acknowledged, welcomed and feared. So the Celts' festive gatherings were held to honour the dead, as well as to promote the endless flow of energy that held the universe in balance.

This year, on race day, Wilf and I drove halfway to Béal Bán, parked the car, and walked through the burial ground at Dún Úrlann. As we walked we could hear music from the beach, and the sound of galloping hooves on hard sand. It was a glorious day, with blue skies and white clouds. Small birds swooped from the fields to the hedges, carrying food to their nestlings. The green sides of the mountains were striped and patched with gold.

As we picked our way between the graves we talked about the first time we'd come to the races, nearly ten years ago, a week after the day we met Mikeen. The weather was clear that year too, and the roads were crowded. Horseboxes and competitors had gathered at one end of the beach and there was a line of cars and trucks parked by the dunes, beside the racetrack. People sitting on the dunes looked out across the curving, mile-long stretch of white sand at the flat, turquoise ocean and the high, blazing sky. White gulls drifted over the waves. In the distance, the three peaks of the headland known as The Three Sisters shimmered in the heat.

As Wilf and I walked towards the dunes, looking for a vantage point, Jimmy and Maria waved to us from a parked van. At the end of the track I could see Mikeen, in his broad-brimmed hat, organising the riders. Wilf and I climbed into the dunes and met Jack's second sister, Máirín, and her family, eating ice creams. Jack was down by the track, checking out the horses. Gamblers were queuing up to bet on certainties that might yet turn out to be delusions.

The horses' coats gleamed. The riders' satin shirts were green and pink and yellow and chequered in diamonds. As Wilf and I found our vantage point and sat down, a baby stumbled onto the track below us, following a beach ball. Stewards shouted and his mum ran out and scooped him back. His little brother, running at her heels, grabbed the ball and kicked it off the track and into the dunes. It was a hard, straight kick and there was a good-natured round of applause. Then everyone concentrated on the starting line.

I've no idea which horse won, or what kind of race it was. All I was aware of was the dazzling rush of colour, and the weight of muscle and bone. They streaked past between us and the ocean, their hooves pounding the hard sand. The horses' coats were white and brown and black and red-brown, the colours of spray and earth and turf and polished chestnuts. White foam flew back from the bits, and dark sand flew up from the hooves. Pink and yellow and chequered satin blurred into a multi-coloured streak, flashing in the sunlight. Seconds later they were past us, thundering on down the track. I blinked and kept looking straight ahead. The air still seemed to vibrate and shimmer with their passing. But in front of me there was only the white line of the beach, the blue line of the turning tide, and the straight line of the distant horizon.

As I write this now, the work of the harvest's going on around Tí Neilli Mhuiris. In some places here you can still see haycocks standing in stone-walled fields so small and steep that machines can't harvest them. But these days the grass is mostly machine-cut and bundled into big, round silage bales, sealed in black plastic. The sound of the work goes on into the night, when the big containers still rattle past on the roads, pulled by tractors. And, even at night, the air smells of dry grass warmed by the sun.

Lughnasa's a time of hard work and deep pleasures. Wilf and I ate the first of our potatoes a fortnight ago, sitting under the willow tree. The north wind had delayed them, but a few days of sunshine brought new life to the stalks. We had the saucepan on the slate table in front of us, a bowl of yellow butter to eat them with, and scallions pulled from the earth and washed at the garden tap. Soon we'll dig a share for Jim and Carmel and take it up the hill as thanks for the seaweed that nourished them. Last night we ate soup made with spinach, garlic, onions and potatoes, flavoured with nutmeg. Later, sitting outside, we watched runner beans and peas curling up their poles, almost ready to be eaten in their turn. The strength of life in leaf and branch is extraordinary. Wilf cut those tall sticks from the hedge a year ago, trimmed them and made them into beanpoles. But the sap still rose in them. By the end of last season, under their load of green pods and crimson flowers, the stripped poles had begun to make leaf and root. If we hadn't pulled them out and stacked them for this year's planting, we'd have started this spring with new hedges sprouting in the middle of the garden.

And as each season follows the next it brings its own smells and sounds, customs and foods. Some foods are newer here than others. Thyme doesn't like the Atlantic winds but marjoram spills out of flowerbeds and roots itself in the paths. Rainbow chard grows yellow and green, with deep, beetroot-coloured veins in its curling, spear-shaped leaves. Self-seeded marigolds give spicy orange petals that flavour sponge cakes made with honey. The flavouring's not traditional, but honey and spices have always been loved here. Gooseberries and rhubarb pies are traditional. And turnips, carrots and onions, and sweet, creamy parsnips. There's earthy beetroot, boiled and eaten cold, with vinegar, on soda bread. And apples, in their season, peeled and chopped, sprinkled with sugar and cloves, covered with pastry lids and baked on flat, tin plates. There's mackerel, bass and pollock, bacon and dark-green cabbage; and pheasant or the odd rabbit if anyone's out with a gun. In autumn and winter there are chutneys and preserves, and jam made with blackberries gathered at the roadsides. And then spring comes round again with the joys of new greens, small peas eaten straight from the pod, and salt-fed lamb.

I remember sitting with a dictionary once, working my way through a medieval text of St Brendan's voyage to find the Isle of the Blessed. Sitting at my desk in a strip-lit library in Dublin, I was sailing along with the monks in their skin naomhóg when I came to a description of an uninhabited island where they found sheep grazing alone. Suddenly I could smell salt in the air, and see cropped grass scoured by Atlantic winds. Men from the Great Blasket once took their sheep to the outlying islands, and left them to graze. They carried the struggling animals up the sheer cliffs on their backs. You had to learn to balance yourself to take the weight. When the grass on one island was grazed, they'd row across and bring the sheep back down again. Then they'd have to rope them together by the feet, and heave them into the naomhóg. Jumping from the slippery rocks to the pitching boats was dangerous; and then the heavy boats, packed with up to fifteen sheep tied together, were rowed to another island. Where they were carried up the cliffs again, and left to continue to fatten on the rich, salty grass. Farmers still graze their sheep out on the islands. The rich meat is a delicacy here in Corca Dhuibhne. It's first eaten at Easter and prized all through the summer.

A couple of years ago Wilf and I were crossing from the Great Blasket to Dún Chaoin by ferry when we saw a small boat, powered by outboard motor, putting out from one of the islands. The man at the tiller was Wilf's friend, Maidhc. Wilf had been trying to text him all day about a music session in the pub. As Maidhc's boat cruised past us, we waved and did concertina miming, and got the message across. Then the ferry held back to let him shoot ahead and bring his passengers to land before we did. Packed into his boat, like noisy adolescents on an outing, were a dozen woolly, bleating, black-faced sheep.

Each year, before the harvest, whole Celtic communities climbed to high places at Lughnasa; it was a celebration of life that had deep religious significance. Huge crowds, tents, music, bonfires, eating, drinking and dancing till dawn. Sexual freedom was encouraged as an expression of fertility, but it was also a festival that celebrated family and community. Extended families met and hung out together; marriages were arranged; animals were bought and sold; and cows and sheep were sacrificed and eaten on the mountaintops at feasts that went on for days. Lugh's story's one of the oldest myths there is.

It imagines harvest time as an epic battle between light and darkness, which frees the crops from the earth and allows us to claim them. And when you watch the race to harvest the crops here before winter, you can understand why.

Over the years, and in different places, there've been different versions of Lugh's story. Here in Corca Dhuibhne he strides up Mount Brandon from the east with his golden spear, and defeats Crom Dubh, 'the crooked, dark one'. His victory's still celebrated every year in the village of Cloghane, on the east side of Mount Brandon. People climb the mountain from the east, light fires and have picnics. But though the festival's celebrated at Lughnasa, the people call it *Domhnach Chruim Dhuibh*, which means 'Crom Dubh's Sunday'. In their version of the story the edges of two contradictory traditions have got blurred.

In the Middle Ages in Ireland, storytellers swapped St Patrick, or St Brendan for Lugh, and made Crom Dubh into a pagan chieftain whom the saints either killed or converted. And in lots of places the Christian legends took over and the pagan myths were forgotten. That's why Mount Brandon's now called after St Brendan. But in twenty-first-century Corca Dhuibhne, even though the name the Celts used for Mount Brandon's been forgotten, there are living echoes of Crom as a powerful god. When old people here insist they're right about something, you still hear them saying '*Dar Chruim*'. Once I asked an old man to translate that for me, and he stopped for a bit, looking puzzled. Then he said he supposed it meant 'by God'. He was right. It means 'by Crom'.

And in some stories it's Crom, the crooked dark one, not Lugh, driving his golden horses, who brings the harvest out of the earth to feed the people. Maybe those stories are memories of tall, fair-haired invaders with horse-drawn chariots who took over the land from small, dark farmers. I don't know. No one does. But I know peoples' instincts don't change. So, just as pagan gods were displaced by Christian saints, I suppose stories about older pagan gods must have been reshaped and retold to make incoming gods more important. Perhaps Lugh defeating Crom is an echo of ancient propaganda, as well as an image of light defeating darkness. 'Our big sun god beat your crooked dark guy.' If it is, the propaganda failed. Both stories survived. The festival of Lughnasa celebrates Lugh's triumph over Crom Dubh. But in Cloghane it's still Crom Dubh's day.

And if you ask people why, they'll tell you that's just how it is. They're aware of the contradictions and they're not fazed by them. To them, what matters is what's there, because it's part of the picture. You pass on what you've received because it's your children's inheritance. What they do with it is up to themselves. All that's required of them is to pass it on in their turn, remembering that no story is unimportant because each sheds light on the rest.

Like the stories of Crom Dubh and Lugh, much of what survives here is fragmented. But if you believe that all things are contained within all other things, fragmentation can intensify the process of understanding. As stories are told and retold, each fragment in itself becomes a focus for refraction, shedding new light, demanding more awareness and stimulating discussion. And there are always contradictions.

One autumn night in Tí Neillí Mhuiris we'd sent round a text asking if anyone fancied some music, and people turned up throughout the evening. Frances Kennedy from Dún Chaoin, who's a great baker, arrived with a tray of Chelsea Buns covered by a check tea towel. I lifted the tea towel and admired the whorls of spicy dough filled with currants, raisins and sultanas and glazed with runny honey. Traditional soda breads and scones are raised with buttermilk and bicarbonate, which, in Ireland, is just called 'bread soda'. But the dough for Chelsea Buns is raised with baker's yeast. So, when I'd piled the buns on a plate, and set it on a bench by the fire, we talked about the recipe. And Frances insisted that baking with yeast wasn't unusual in Dún Chaoin. 'My mother used it,' she said. There was a chorus of disbelief. '*Yeast*? She used yeast? Where did she get it?' 'Some shop in Dún Chaoin, I don't remember. Or maybe she got it in Dingle.' Other people in the room were adamant. 'There was no shop in Dún Chaoin sold yeast in your mother's time.'

259

The argument flowed cheerfully on as people wolfed the buns. I poured tea and made coffee. Frances was holding her ground. 'Well, the women in Dún Chaoin used yeast, I remember it.' Someone from this side of the mountain slapped a hand on the bench. 'Sure, the women in Dún Chaoin always had something the rest of us hadn't!' There was laughter, and the talk turned to John Kennedy's bees who'd provided the honey. Then someone doubled back and demanded to know what the Dún Chaoin women had baked with their yeast. Details are important here. Specificity matters; each note's place in a piece of music, each twist and turn in a story. 'They didn't bake Chelsea Buns?' Of course they didn't. Frances got the recipe in a cookbook. 'What did they bake with it, then?' 'N'fheadair, I don't know, bread, I suppose.' 'Bread!!?' There was another chorus of disbelief, and Frances threw her hands up, laughing. Then, as the last of the buns were eaten, someone started a tune on a whistle. Musicians wandered into the other room to wash honey glaze off their fingers under the kitchen tap. And the fiddles and concertinas joined the music.

Later that evening, about ten o'clock, Jack, who'd been sitting by the fire, got up to go home. Helen, who'd been playing the whistle, stood up too, and said she'd give him a lift down the hill. Jack shook his head and went to the door. As he opened it, I heard Helen laughing. Outside, waiting patiently by the step, were Jack's two dogs, the cat and three hens. Jack looked down at them and didn't miss a beat. 'I'd say they were bored below without me,' he said. 'They came up to walk me home.'

The story about the talking cat in Cathar na gCat, who asked for a present from Dingle, must have come from occasions like that. So must Puss In Boots, and the talking fox in the Russian story about the Firebird. They belong to communities in which animals aren't fashion accessories or providers of 'unconditional love'. Instead they're fellow creatures with their own lives and personalities. Once they were gods. And they're creatures we can learn from, because their experience of the world we share with them may be deeper and richer than ours.

I remember that once I asked Jack how he taught his dogs to work with sheep and cattle. He said not all dogs are apt for the job. But when they are, he doesn't teach them. The dogs teach each other. When we first met Spot she was learning from Sailor. Since then I've watched her train her own pups, from birth to the time they go off to learn on another farm. Jack only has work for one dog now, plus a kind of part-time job for Mike George's dog, Rover, who decided a while ago that he fancied going freelance. The pups are born in the hayshed or the woodshed. Spot decides herself where she'll have them, behind a woodpile, in a dark corner, or under an old door leaning against the wall. Several of her litters were fathered by Mikey, Mrs Manning's dog from over the road. Mikey was a beautiful dog, with a black and white head and dark brown intelligent eyes. He was a good worker but an irritable father, who snapped at the pups if they came near him. As far as he was concerned, if he wasn't up in the fields his job was to lie outside the shed, guarding the entrance, while Spot did the rest.

Mikey died a few years ago, and Rover, who fathered Spot's last litter, is more easy-going. Rover's a brindled dog, with blue eyes. He puts a lot of effort into keeping the hens in one place but, when his back's turned, they always regroup according to their own notions. When the pups are old enough to play in the garden he indulges them, letting them jump on his back and worry his tail. But it's still Spot who trains them.

A week or so after they're born, she follows the tractor to the fields again herself, leaving the pups in the shed. If you look in when she's not there you never see them. She teaches them to stay hidden. A week or so later, they're allowed to stagger almost to the door; the largest and bravest will growl and squeak if you look in, and they'll all retreat to the woodpile if your foot crosses the threshold. After that, you see them sitting in the doorway, staring up the road, waiting for mum. By then, though they're still suckling, Spot's getting tired of them. Soon they're allowed out onto the concrete path that leads from the sheds to the garden, and she's back on the plinth by the road, or lying round the corner, by the front door.

But the pups never cross the invisible lines laid down for them. It's not a matter of chasing them back if they stray. Somehow, she indicates where the lines are drawn, and when they're allowed to pass them. And, till they're old enough to fend for themselves, whether or not she's present, they never disobey. In the fields, it's the same process. The young dogs follow and watch, and learn by imitation, and, when the time comes, they pass on the skills they've learnt from their elders.

A few weeks ago I woke about five in the morning. There was a sliver of moon still hanging above the clouds, and the world outside the window was silver-grey. I got out of bed to go to the loo. As I came back, I saw a hare slowly circling Tí Neillí Mhuiris. There are folktales here in which circling hares are witches in disguise. In myths they're gods, or servants of the goddess who bring messages from the moon. The hare in the garden was as big as a small dog, with powerful back legs and slanting eyes. The fur on his back was pale gold. His chest and belly were white. I moved from window to window, watching him. He moved slowly, turning his head from side to side, intently focused on single blades of grass or patches of herbs. He wasn't eating. He touched them with his nose and then moved on. Every so often he stopped and sat back on his haunches. I watched his short ears turning as he monitored his world. When he turned the corner of the house, I could see marks left in the dew on the grass by his feet. Then, as I crossed from one window to another, he must have caught a movement behind the glass. He stopped, his head turned, and he looked straight at me. His slanting eyes were pale. I don't know if he comes here each night, or where he goes in daytime. I don't think he was a witch or a messenger from the goddess. But, meeting his remote stare in the waning moonlight, it was easy to believe that the silver-grey garden outside my window wasn't mine, or even Neillí's. It belonged to him.

I first read about Lugh, the sun god, as a child, colouring in pictures in a storybook. Over thirty years ago, on my first morning at Mrs Hurley's, that myth, the need to create it, and the impulse to pass it on, began to make a different kind of sense to me. Looking up at Mount Brandon, I'd recognised links between Lugh's story and human fear of darkness. But it wasn't till we came to live here that I began to realise its place in an ancient world view in which the turning wheel of the year offers an image of life within death.

This year when Wilf and I made our way to the Béal Bán races we walked through the burial ground at Dún Úrlann. In the distance we could hear the sound of hooves drumming on sand. It was a glorious day, with blue skies and white clouds. Small birds swooped from the fields to the hedges, carrying food to their nestlings. There was music on the beach, and the smell of salt on the wind. And we passed by the foot of Mikeen Sullivan's grave.

We were in London when Mikeen died, so we didn't follow his coffin. We didn't hear of his death till it was too late. But when we came back we heard the stories of his funeral. The mourners came from every parish, and from England: neighbours; men who'd worked on the sites with him; horse-dealers and riders; and men he'd met at the fairs. The people followed his coffin from Ballyferriter to Dún Úrlann. And it was carried on a hearse pulled by horses.

As long as people have lived, the seasons have turned, crops have been planted, beasts have been hunted, livestock's been reared, and boats have put out to sea. People marry and women bear children. Children grow up and have children of their own. Old people are cared for. The sick are nursed. The dead are remembered with stories and carved stones. The living are comforted with visions of rebirth. And no one's ever known what will happen next.

12

Dancing Through Darkness

The season that follows Lughnasa is Samhain. It's the dark, cold time of year when the landscape changes, the wind drives in from the north and west, and Atlantic storms hurl white spray high onto the clifftops. Sitting by the fire in Tí Neillí Mhuiris, with the flames leaping, scones in the oven and a pot of tea by the hearthstone, the contrast between the comfort indoors and the wildness outside is one of the great joys of living here.

Winter ends our year, but the ancient Celts' new year

began on the last night of October, the turning point between Lughnasa and Samhain. Nowadays, most people who dress up as ghosts and ghouls for Hallowe'en have no idea that its name means 'the night of the spirits', or that trick or treating's an echo of Celtic ritual. Here it celebrated an annual turning point when the spirits of the dead returned to the homes they'd once lived in, and were welcomed with feasting and fires. Mainly so they wouldn't get offended and revenge themselves on their descendants.

I remember being astonished when I first went to London that people said Hallowe'en was an import from America. It may have returned to England from America fairly recently. But it's rooted in Europe's Celtic heritage, and in Ireland it's always been celebrated with bonfires, candles stuck in turnip heads and masked visits to the neighbours. Though, having said that, I remember my own first Hallowe'en mask was a cardboard Mickey Mouse. I wore it with a black polo neck and tights, white gloves, and a long tail made of plaited wool stiffened with wire from a straightened-out coat hanger. It was raining that night and my mother made me add a dark-grey duffle coat, with the hood up, which spoiled the effect. On the other hand, I liked the sinister way my black tail showed under my coat when I turned away from my neighbours' doors with a pocketful of apples and monkey nuts. I was a mouse you wouldn't risk offending.

Light and heat matter in winter. For thousands of years, living flames have been images of life itself. When we first came to Tí Neillí Mhuiris, I remember we had discussions about how we'd heat the house. We got advice on different systems and made price comparisons between oil and electricity. And, in the meantime, we lit fires in Neillí's fireplace. I remember Jack coming into the room one day and stretching his hand to the warmth. It was chilly outside and the fire had burnt low. So I threw another sod on it and we watched red flames curl round black turf as the new sod took life from the old ones. Wilf was there too, and we stood in contented silence as the flames began to crackle and burn yellow. Then Jack said what all three of us were thinking. 'You'd like to be looking at it.'

We've kept Neillí's fire; when I need a break from writing I walk across the room and throw a sweet-smelling sod of turf onto the hearth, to make the flames dance and light glimmer on the hearthstone; and in the new room there's a solid-fuel stove. It's not the most efficient, or cost-effective system, but gnarled branches of fuchsia burn well when the sap's dried out of them, and the ash trees throw down rotten branches for kindling. And there's plenty of heat to be had from an extra sweater. It'd be hard to live here now without the smell of turf and the sight of the flames. Some people shrug when they hear that, and say they suppose we like the old ways. Which may be a polite way of not saying they think we're daft. And, admittedly, there are occasions when you could see their point if they did say it. There was, for example, the chimney-cleaning episode.

It happened in our first autumn in Tí Neillí Mhuiris, when we'd decided to clean the chimney before the winter. Wilf, who'd been reading a book of mine about folk customs, announced that all we needed was a furze bush, a stone and a decent length of rope. The fire had gone out overnight. So I cleared the grate while he took a pair of secateurs and went to find a furze bush. Furze, or gorse, is the prickly bush that smells of coconut in summer, when its yellow flowers are heated by the sun. But in the autumn, when the flowers are gone, it's just prickly. And difficult to cut. So, after some consideration, and quite a lot of cursing, Wilf extended his list of requirements to include a bow saw and a pair of leather gauntlets. Eventually, having cut his furze bush, he tied it to a length of rope, carefully calculated to reach from the chimney pot down to the hearthstone. After that, he tied a stone to the other end of the rope, heavy enough to drag it down the chimney. And after that, inevitably, he went for a ladder. I hate it when he does that; it always ends up with me on the ground shouting inane things like 'be careful'.

When the ladder was positioned against the end of the house there was a pause while I looked in the opposite direction and Wilf climbed up, over the gutter, and edged his way up the roof till he reached the chimney-stack. Then there were three failed attempts to throw the rope up to him without braining him with the stone or felling him with the furze bush. Eventually he caught the rope, looped most of it over his shoulder, took hold of the furze bush in readiness, and dropped the stone down the chimney. I then galloped into the room, where I'd already pushed back the furniture and covered things in newspaper. And there was the stone, tied to the rope's end, lying on the hearthstone. The other end of the rope, I hoped, was still tied to the furze bush. I squinted up the chimney. High above, I could see daylight. I yelled that I'd got the rope's end and the daylight vanished. This meant that Wilf had put the furze bush in position. Now all I had to do was drag it through the chimney pot and down the flue, collecting all the soot on the way down.

It wasn't a completely ineffective system. The first bit was the dodgiest, because the chimney pot was narrow. But once I'd dragged the bush into the flue, the compressed, prickly branches opened out, and the pulling got easier. The bush itself blocked the falling soot it was scraping from the sides of the chimney. The rope, however, was increasingly filthy. And halfway down, the bush got stuck, so I had to reach up as far as I could to get more purchase. For several minutes, with my arms lost in darkness, I pulled on the rope and nothing happened. I was sure that if I jerked it too hard the knot would give way and we'd have a permanent furze bush up the chimney. I had visions of having to light a fire to burn it out, which would probably have burnt the house down. Then I remembered another description in the book I'd been daft enough to let Wilf read; in some places they'd drop a goose down the chimney and his wildly fluttering wings would sweep the soot down. Why hadn't we tried that one?

Frantically, I squinted up into the black hole and gave the rope a desperate jerk. There was a flurry of choking dust and coils of heavy rope suddenly shot down onto the hearthstone. Seconds later, the bush landed in the grate and rolled out into the room, scattering soot all around it.

So the next thing to do was to carry it out of the house. But the bush and the rope were caked with loose soot. I tried wrapping the bush in newspaper but the razor-sharp prickles defeated me. In the end I gathered the rope against my chest and walked across the room with the bush held out at arm's length. Where it swung gently from the rope's end, coating everything in the room in a layer of thin black dust.

Outside, Wilf was still clinging to the chimneystack, and Jack was at the gate, looking up at him. As I appeared, he transferred his gaze to me. It was only later that I realised what I must have looked like. My shirt was filthy. I was clutching a pile of grimy rope tied to a blackened furze bush. My arms were black to the elbows and my face and hair were sooty. Wilf edged down the roof, clambered over the gutter and down the ladder. An explanation seemed in order so he told Jack what we'd done, ending with '. . . we thought we'd stick to the old ways, and it really works, doesn't it?' There was a pause while Jack looked at us. Wilf worries that people here don't always follow his English accent, so he went through it again, ending with '. . . so we used the furze bush. To clean the chimney. Isn't that what they used to do here?' Jack shook his head. 'Ah, no,' he said. I dumped my filthy coil of rope on the ground and waited to be educated. Clearly there was yet another folk custom, specific to the area. 'So you wouldn't drop a furze bush down the chimney?' said Wilf. 'Or a goose?' said I. 'Ah, no,' said Jack. 'We wouldn't. We'd borrow Mike George's brushes.'

Chimney cleaning's just one of the tasks that need doing here before winter. In the past, mackerel was salted, vegetables were stored and the fruits of the summer were converted into food for the barren months ahead. People stocked up on flour and oatmeal, tea and sugar, paying for them with whatever money they'd make by selling stock, or fish, or spare produce. Careful housewives scraped and saved to provide presents, and special food for Christmas dinner. Having enough, and eking it out through the dark months, was vital for survival. In the past, people here shared with their neighbours as things got increasingly scarce. And the tradition of sharing's as strong as it ever was in Corca Dhuibhne. One Christmas, Wilf and I were both ill here. Several of our neighbours offered to drive over to us on Christmas day with a share of their own Christmas dinner.

The tradition of midwinter feasting's ancient. To the Celts it was about sacrifice; at a time when nothing grew, they shared and ate the best of what they had, to demonstrate confidence in the future. For them, the dark season was also the time when the Good Goddess was pregnant with the promise of springtime, and longer, lighter days. In the Christian tradition it's the season when the Virgin Mary carried her child to Bethlehem, to be born as the light of the world. And all across the world, lights and fires are symbols of hope and celebration in seasons of darkness. But in the twenty-first century, statistics show our highest levels of stress, loneliness, and debt-related suicide when Christmas lights are strung across city streets and tinsel glitters in shop windows. Somewhere along the way, we've lost touch with the meaning of our rituals and symbols. But I think that if we reach out for the meaning we can re-engage with the sense of empowerment they were developed to inspire.

If you cross the mountain to Dingle on Christmas Eve you'll see lights shining all round you. In every house here there's a light in each window. As you drive back west along the winding roads, clusters of lights mark the presence of villages. And higher up, where the dark bulk of the mountains shows against the sky, single flames glimmer in farmhouse windows. In the past, the doors here were all left unlocked on Christmas Eve, and fires burnt all night on the hearthstones. The open doors, the fires and the candles in the windows are all traditional rituals. And they're echoes of older rituals that brought light to the darkest months of the year in Corca Dhuibhne.

These days the lights in the windows here are often electric; but once they were specially-bought Christmas candles, set in jars full of sand that the children brought up from the beach. And in some households the old glass or stoneware jars, that once held jam or marmalade, are still carefully kept. They come out at Christmas to be wrapped in coloured paper and set on the windowsills. And boxes of the tall, red candles, big enough to burn each night through the Christmas season, still appear in shops here in December. They offer warmth and shelter to Joseph and Mary on their way to Bethlehem, where, in the Christian story, Christ was born in a stable because there was no room at the inn. It's a tradition handed down from one generation to another, and remembered all over Ireland.

When I was a child in Dublin, Christmas was about setting up the crib. We had a Christmas tree as well, anchored in the coal bucket, or in the bigger turf basket. And there was holly. And paper chains put up by my father and brothers; the twisted lengths of crêpe paper reached from the picture rails to the central light fitting, turning the dining-room ceiling into a coloured canopy. And there were other family rituals as well; my aunt's arrival on the train from Enniscorthy with the turkey and the ham in her luggage; big, square loaves of white bread with black crusts, to be turned into breadcrumbs for the stuffing; my mother stirring the pudding on the stove; two Christmas cakes on silver cardboard plinths, waiting for their marzipan and sugar-icing toppings, and for the robins and little Eskimos made of chalk.

The house smelt of nutmeg and brown sugar. I remember helping to hang holly. I remember one sister painting Christmas cards and the other making jelly for trifle; and myself sitting at the kitchen table, wrapped in one of my mother's aprons, polishing plates that only came out for Christmas. And I remember the year my brothers told me my present was seventh from the top of the pile they'd stacked under the Christmas tree. I spent hours counting down from the top of that pile of six presents. In my defence, I was only four years old at the time.

But more than anything else, I remember the crib. It was a traditional nativity scene, about nine inches high, arranged on a table near the tree against the backdrop of a stable that folded out like a three-part screen. I don't know when I took over the job of setting up the crib. But I do remember it as an intensely solitary pleasure. Each year I unpacked it from a two-tier Black Magic chocolate box, opened with a scarlet tassel. I think the pottery figures came from two different, incomplete sets, probably one from Galway and one from Enniscorthy. So I had two choices for the virgin and several possible shepherds. And five wise kings in perfect condition, from which, each year, I chose three.

I remember brooding over which figures to use. One set was more crudely made than the other, but the crude one had the best colours; Joseph had a grass-green tunic and a brown cloak, and Mary wore white and sky blue. The figures in the other set were more detailed, based on Italian renaissance woodcarvings; their clothes were edged with gilt and painted with stars. Most years I chose the dumpier, plainer figures for Joseph, Mary and the baby, and used a mixture for the shepherds. One shepherd came with a lamb on his shoulder; another had a set of pipes. Choosing the kings was easy because the taller, more aristocratic figures, with their sharply-sculpted robes and golden crowns, seemed most impressive. One carried a little box studded with painted red stones. The animals were easiest. I just used them all. And in the background there were cows and ducks and dogs and pigs and sheep from my brother's discarded toy farm. Some were plastic. Others were die-cast lead. I have two of the lead sheep still, here in Tí Neillí Mhuiris. Every Christmas they tower over the other, wooden figures in the crib here on Neillí's mantelpiece. I suppose that, technically, they're still my brother's, but I reckon no jury would convict me after that thing with the pile of presents.

Then one day, when I was about nine, someone gave me a book called *My Paper Crib*. Each page had a design to be painted, cut out, and made into an elegant, modern three-dimensional figure. In the week before Christmas my father painted them with poster paints, in rich, chalky colours. Then he cut them out, curled, folded and glued them. I remember waiting impatiently while the figures stood on the mantelpiece with their skirts held in place by paperclips while the glue set overnight. In those twenty-four hours my choices had expanded and I was longing to set up the crib. But when I came to it, the new figures wouldn't mix with the old ones; the design, style and materials were too different. In the end I had to choose. So that year the old figures stayed in their boxes and the new ones stood on the table, allowing no compromise. On Christmas Eve I tried lighting a candle by them. But my mother pointed out that they were made of paper, so we plugged in a table lamp instead. In our Dublin city semi, flames were primarily seen as a health hazard.

But in the past, living flames on the hearth were seen as the heart of the household. In Ireland there's a tradition of covering the turf fire with ashes at night, raking it out in the morning, and using the living embers under the ash to rekindle it. My father told me his grandmother in Connemara had a prayer she said each night when she covered her fire. I remember him teaching it to me in Dublin when I was a child, though the fire in that house was carefully raked out each night and the grate was cold in the morning. The prayer was in Irish.

Coigilím an tine seo anocht mar a choigilíonn Críost cách.
Muire ar dhá cheann an tí agus Bríd ina lár.
Geach a bhfuil d'aspail agus aingil i gCathair na nGrást
Go ndiníg díon do'n tig agus dá bhfuil ann go lá.

I save this fire tonight as Christ saves all.
Mary at the two ends of the house and Bríd in the centre.
However many apostles and angels there are in the City
    of Grace
May they make a roof for the house, and all in it, till
    daybreak.

In English, covering and rekindling a fire is called 'smooring'. In some houses, fires were kept alive on the hearth for years. There's a story about a family that had to leave Ireland for America at the beginning of the twentieth century. The grandmother couldn't bear to put her fire out. So she covered it with ashes, said her prayer, and closed the door behind her. She said the women of the house had kept that fire for seven generations and she wouldn't be the one to let it die. I save the fire now in Tí Neillí Mhuiris as my great-grandmother saved hers in Connemara. A few years ago a neighbour here in Corca Dhuibhne told me his grandmother had the same prayer as hers. Neillí would have had one too. And her mother before her.

In the folk tradition, Mary, the mother of Christ, and Bríd, the Irish saint, protect the sleeping household until daybreak. They're echoes of the Good Goddess – the 'strongest and most energetic of women', destroyers of darkness, and powerful shields in battle. All three are images of fertility, healing and hope; and for thousands of years the same ideas have been shaped and reshaped in their stories. Seeds waken to the pressure of Danú's naked feet; flowers spring up when Bríd's cloak touches the earth; when Mary's cloak's hung on a rosemary bush the flowers become sky blue. They control the earth. And all three of them are linked with light and fire. The echoes resonate from one tradition to another; the Good Goddess marries Lugh, the sun god; Mary's child brings light into the world; Bríd lights a sacred flame that's kept burning for centuries. And those stories are still heard here in Corca Dhuibhne. As a child setting up the crib, I wanted old images to coexist with new ones, making a deeper, richer whole. Now I'm living in a community where that's part of the fabric of life.

Nollaig na mBan means 'Women's Christmas.' It's celebrated on 6 January, when the men take over the household duties and women of all ages get together and party. They meet at home, or go out in groups, to eat, sing, drink, dance and generally hang out together. The village pubs and restaurants are full all night, and the dancing often spills onto the street. Grannies and aunties dance with little girls, friends get up and sing songs together, and houses are full of music. Nollaig na mBan used to be celebrated all over Ireland, and in lots of places it still is. It's a meeting of generations and a time for sharing. And its roots are in the ancient belief that winter's a time to celebrate the goddess.

I remember the first time I joined a table of women in a candlelit pub in Ballyferriter, for Nollaig na mBan. The singing had already begun. Everyone was dressed to party. Which left me feeling pretty conspicuous, as Wilf was still working on Tí Neilli Mhuiris and I'd spent the day up a ladder, helping him to paint walls. But no one blinked an eye at my paint-stained hands, with the nails worn down by sandpaper, or my least-grubby jeans. I was introduced all round and people shoved up to make room.

The barman was carrying trays of drinks and platters of food from the kitchen. A couple of older women, in seats closest to the fire, were keeping an eye on a group of little girls, dressed in their best, who were already jigging to the music. It was a cheerful, welcoming night of shared talk and laughter. And when the dancing started, it was the oldest women who were first onto the floor.

I can't remember if that was the first time I saw Cáit Chosaí dancing, but I've seen her many times since. Wherever there's music she's up on her feet. I've even seen her dance to the music of the organ as she walks out of a church. The first money Cáit ever earned she spent on a bike, so she could cycle to the dancehalls. She grew up at a time when the grip of the Roman Catholic Church on the community was rigid here, and priests often broke in on dances with threats of hellfire. 'They'd come into Muiríoch Hall and they'd scatter the dancers. They'd drive us out the back and through the river!' 'They would! And they'd break into the houses cursing us.' 'He'd be reading out of his book.' 'He'd be in one door and we'd all be out the other!'

The women laugh now when they remember it, but at the time it must have been frightening. The priests tried to ban music and dancing at the crossroads too, and at the patterns by the holy wells. Mostly they succeeded, and for most of the twentieth century the Irish state was dominated by the Church's ideal of celibacy. So authorities' attitudes towards sexuality, and towards women, became more and more warped. Yet nothing stopped the dances in Corca Dhuibhne. Jack's sister Nóirín can remember girls cycling through the dark to the dancehalls with high heels hanging round their neck. I've heard that same story from almost every woman of her generation.

And beneath a compliant surface, women here never lost a sense of their own identities. Cáit Chosaí's generation grew up with the tradition of arranged marriages. Some friend or relation would act as matchmaker, and couples might spend very little time together before their wedding. But traditionally, a girl could send an offer to a man just as easily as a man could send one to a woman. And if a man married into a woman's people's land, like Neilli's Paddy did, he was expected to bring a dowry.

Cáit Chosaí sent an offer to the man she married. She talks about it still. 'I chose my husband. I said no one else would satisfy me, and if I didn't get him, I'd go to America.' She sent him a message by her aunt. He was twelve years older than Cáit, and had 'two left feet' on the dance floor. But 'he was kind and good humoured, and he was good company.' And they had a long and happy marriage. Cáit's in her eighties now, still clear minded and confident. And it still only takes two bars of a tune to get her up dancing.

Corca Dhuibhne rears powerful women. I have neighbours who grew up without electricity or running water, on isolated farms, doing back-breaking work. They led lives that would exhaust the average woman today. They looked after families, milked cows, made butter, cared for calves, raised poultry and baked their bread in iron pots at the side of an open fire. As children, they walked barefoot to school. As adults they often worked barefoot too, and helped the men in the fields. I once asked a neighbour how a woman coped if a man was hurt and couldn't work. She told me she got up sooner and went to bed later. 'Whoever did it, the work still had to be done.'

I've often heard younger women here envy their mothers' and grandmothers' spiritual and emotional strength. They call them 'mighty women' and admire their serenity and resilience. Those women had an inner strength that kept them going, an intuitive sense of balance and a deep belief in God. One powerful touchstone for their strength is the way their feistiness survived the twisted values imposed here by the Church.

I remember a woman called Máirín na Yanks Ní Mhurchú, who owned a shop near Mrs Hurley's. She was raised by two aunts who'd come back from America – which is why people called her Máirín na Yanks. I used to buy chocolate from her when I first came here, and sometimes we'd meet on the roads, picking black-berries. A few years ago, shortly before she died, she was interviewed for an Irish language television series. It was called *Bibeanna*, which is the Irish word for the wraparound aprons women here used to wear in the house and the farmyard. They were made of dark fabric, patterned with little flowers. I remember watching the series on television and thinking that Máirín's quiet voice hadn't changed since I'd first heard it. Sitting by her fire, wrapped in her flowery apron, she described her life, looking back on her childhood and the years she'd spent in her shop. She talked about the pleasure she took in the company of neighbours who'd drop in for a chat. Then she summed it all up in a sentence. 'I'm calm and easy in myself; I take each day as it comes and I keep my door open.'

When I first came here I heard stories about Máirín na Yanks' aunts being so strict they'd hardly let her leave the house. She said it herself in that interview. 'I had no youth,' she said, 'I cried myself to sleep many a night. I think the local women were sorry for me.' Once she overheard a neighbour asking her aunts not to be so hard on her. But it was no use. When Máirín was growing up here, the priests literally dragged the girls away from the boys if they saw them together. Máirín never married. Her aunts wouldn't let her have a boyfriend. So her whole life was spent behind the shop counter. In that television interview, she wondered if perhaps she'd been too accepting. 'You can put up with too much,' she said. And looking back, she thought she had. Yet she ended her life 'calm and easy in herself'. And she always smiled when you came through her door.

In the years I've lived here, I've heard other women talk about that repression. Their faces twist when they remember sex-obsessed priests and nuns. And rituals like 'churching', when they had to stand in church holding candles while prayers were said to 'cleanse' them after childbirth. But their own belief in God is personal. 'It's in my blood,' they say, 'it's inside me.' They're devout, but they don't see faith as tied to the Church, or church-going. And they always come back to the concept of balance. 'There are good priests and bad priests,' they say, 'but they should be let marry.' 'Celibacy isn't natural.' 'It's not.' 'And they shouldn't be taught that they're above the rest of us. It's not right.' Other voices chip in. They speak quietly, like Máirín na Yanks, but they speak with authority. 'All God wants is for us to live well and to harm no one.'

Woman's Christmas is important in Corca Dhuibhne.

So is the Wran's Day, which happens on 26 December, just after the winter solstice. They're as much a part of the holiday season here as Christmas Day itself. If you study folklore or anthropology, you learn that the Wran's Day belongs to a tradition that stretches back to the first people who came here, thousands of years before Christianity. Its name's a corruption of the English word 'wren', and in Irish it's *Lá an Dreoilín*. There's endless research on the Wran's Day, and suggestions that *dreoilín*, the word for wren, comes from *draoi-éan*, 'druid's bird'. It's linked to ancient midwinter festivals and shamanism, when a shared web of ideas and information was accessed like a form of internet powered by human energy, and to later folk traditions like Straw Boys and Guisers. Its rituals belong to a dream state beyond stories, or even words, when there were just images and rhythms. But if you turn up in Dingle on 26 December, what you'll see is one big party.

Basically, the town gets taken over by musicians and dancers. In the past, the boys back west used to dress up in rags and old coats turned inside out. They'd smear soot on their faces, or wear masks, and go from house to house, playing music and asking for pennies 'to bury the wran'. Then they'd use the money to buy food and drink and throw a dance. Earlier still, live wrens used to be hunted and killed and carried in procession. Earlier than that, at huge ritual gatherings, kings offered themselves to be killed at the turn of the year, in an extreme version of sacrificing the best you've got in times of scarcity. Through the nineteenth and twentieth centuries, the Church did its best to suppress the Wran's Day. But it never succeeded; and its ancient, wordless rhythms are still felt here every year.

Some kids still walk the roads in costumes here back west, and turn up at their neighbours' houses to dance in the kitchen. Each separate group's called a 'wran'. You hear the creak of the gate and the rattle of a drum outside the window. Then tattered figures with masked and painted faces crowd into the house, disguised in their granny's aprons, padded with rolled-up socks; or their dad's pyjamas, tied with rope and stuffed into wellingtons. As they come into the room, accordion players pull their masks down over their faces and whistle players push them onto their foreheads; the smaller figures giggle and shuffle. Then someone gives a note and the little group breaks into a jig or a polka. But these days most people head for Dingle instead and join the rival parades that march and dance through the streets playing music. Máire Begley blames it on the carpets. 'The real Wran went out the door the day the carpets came into the houses. No one wants mud on the floors nowadays. That's why they all go in to Dingle!'

The Wran's Day in Dingle is famous. Nowadays the

collections are for charities, and the wrans compete to see who can raise the most money on the streets and in the pubs. Different tunes belong to particular streets, and each wran carries its own banner. They march wearing different colours, green and gold, crimson and white, and chequered white and blue. Each wran's led by a prancing horse with a wooden head and snapping jaws. They're echoes of Lugh and his fiery stallions. And of the goddess, one of whose names was Epona, Mother of Mares. The horses' cloth bodies, stretched on wooden frames, hang from the shoulders of the marchers. Behind them are jostling figures in high, pointed masks, whirling skirts and woven breastplates, made from oat straw. They march in line, beating drums and playing fifes and whistles. The golden skirts swing in time to the music as the horses whirl and caper in front of the marchers, and dart through the crowds that follow them. The traditional carved wooden heads and the straw costumes are beautiful. And slightly sinister. Under the straw masks, faces are painted in stripes, or blackened. Eyes gleam through painted eye holes. One horse's snapping teeth are the dentures of a dead man who used to dance in him.

And weaving through the crowd are other dancers. Figures with rubber pigs' heads, in high heels and paint-spattered boiler suits. Skeletons with padded buttocks and breasts. Wolves in wraparound Aviators. Farmers with soot-smeared faces dance past in blue wigs wreathed in tinsel. Grannies wear beards and flashing Santa hats. Onlookers scream as they're dragged into the street and chased by the snapping horses. People stand in doorways and lean out of windows, throwing coins. As each wran swings by, through the streets and in and out of the pubs, scattered groups are left behind, laughing and taking photographs. A few years ago four figures in business suits wearing huge rubber Richard Nixon heads were dancing to a fiddle outside a supermarket. A few steps away, ignoring them, two middle-aged women were chatting. And outside the church, watched by a small, pink fairy, a skeleton in bunny ears was dancing round a handbag.

On frosty winter nights in Corca Dhuibhne, the sky's alive with glimmering stars. As you climb the hill to Tí Neillí Mhuiris, the warm lights in the village are lost below you. Darkness grows deeper as the road curves round the mountain. In fields on either side of you, cows huddle in the gateways. They breathe and snort in the darkness, reaching for mouthfuls of silage. Beyond galvanised iron gates, starlight gleams on frost-hardened mud that's been carved into ruts by their hooves. Stars and planets shimmer above you. On your right is the presence of the mountain. On your left, the dark sky curves over the valley. Where the sky meets the ocean, starlight glimmers faintly on the waves. At Christmas time, as you climb higher still, the stars are echoed in pinpricks of flame all around you; high above on the mountain and scattered below in the valley, lights burn in the windows, calling the traveller home.

From the brow of the hill I can see lights in Tí Neillí Mhuiris. Then, as I turn down the steep road that drops down to the house, they're lost behind Paddy's ash trees. The bare branches strain towards the house; their shapes are carved by a hundred years of winter wind blowing from the north. I walk towards the door under shuddering branches. Inside, between the stone walls and the curved timber ceiling, the house feels like a cave. Red firelight and yellow candlelight touch stone floors and creamy-grey painted walls. I stir the fire, the flame leaps up. New sods take life from the old ones. When I make tea and sit by the fire, the room's crowded with memories. Some are my own. Some have been shared with me.

I remember voices. Voices at the door here, greetings and laughter and people crowding in from the cold. Louis singing by the window. Frances Kennedy throwing up her hands in the heat of an argument: 'There was no shop in Dún Chaoin sold yeast in your mother's time.' 'There was, and I remember it!' 'There was not!' Laughter, singing and gossip. Neillí's box of biscuits under the bed. Paddy's dog sitting at the table. Spot eating crab claws; the cat that ate cabbage; the talking cat up on Cathar na gCat; and Jack's three red hens here, waiting by the door. Neillí's crow of delight at Paddy's stories: '*Céad míle glóir' le Dia!*' she'd say, 'a hundred thousand glories to God!' The voices echo and resonate down the years. Music sounds against stone. Alice raises her glass to Ray. Dancers' feet strike the floor. The room smells of turf smoke and apple cake, and firelight paints the walls. Breandán 'ac Gearailt's father, Jeaic, sang songs here. And Séan de hÓra. And dozens of other neighbours that came in to talk and sing. Neillí sang her own songs, about the rent man and the cost of food. She baked her bread in an iron pot here, and carried water from the spring. And Jim George ran in through the door with her pension and couldn't see the fireplace for the smoke. Con and Lís sat by this fire and stirred the embers. So did Biddy. And Neillí's mother, Bríghid. So did Lasse. Bríghid was waked here, and her coffin was carried out the door. And Emer walked the floor here with her newborn baby in her arms.

The night of our first party here I was dazzled by the idea of all those memories, held between these walls. Now that I've lived here longer, I'm aware of something even more extraordinary. Outside Neillí's door – rooted in customs of the community, and the landscape that sustains it – are older, more impersonal memories, linking the lives lived in this house with the ancient life of the peninsula. Reaching back in time beyond even the people

of the goddess Danú, they offer a deep sense of empowerment, based on shared energy and effort.

Tonight as I scooped the ashes over the embers I
remembered a saying of my mother's, picked up from
her own mother, my Enniscorthy granny. She used it
when life got hard. 'Ah well, if we live through the winter
the Divil wouldn't kill us in the summer!' At the time, I
liked the sound of it, but I didn't know what it meant.
Now I do. It's an echo of a time when surviving through
the dark months left you feeling empowered to do
anything. It was a time when people lived their lives as
part of communities that stood or fell together in the
hard times. It has lessons for the lives we're leading now.

Last year, on the streets of Dingle, I watched a dancing
figure in a straw skirt and a painted paper mask. I don't
know if it was a man or a woman. The feet were in heavy
boots and the hands wore outsize gardening gloves. The
head was crowned with horns. The dance was a little,
circular, shuffling jig. Three steps forward, two back and
then three steps forward. Then the dancer whirled round,
and the circle began again. And from behind me, I heard
a bellow of answering voices. 'Fair play to you! Keep at
it! We never died a winter yet!'

This year, as the nights have grown cold, Wilf's chopped
apples and onions for chutney, and flavoured it with
fennel from the garden. The yellow fennel's powdered
away to dust now, leaving skeletal, silver seed pods on

bleached, bony stalks. Their faint, spicy smell fills the house when they're thrown on the fire. Packed into glass jars, the flavours of the food will mingle over time, each adding its own goodness to our nourishment this winter. We sleep between stone walls, protected by straining ash trees. And here on Neillí's hearthstone, living embers are warm under the ashes.

Afterword

The Music of What Happens

There's a story about Fionn Mac Cumhaill and his warriors hunting the hills of Ireland. They chase the deer from dawn to dusk and then make camp to eat, drink and make music. As they sit by the fire, between tunes and talk, Fionn asks his companions a question. 'What's the best music in the world?' One says it's the cry of the cuckoo. Another says it's the ring of a spear on a shield. Someone suggests the baying of a pack of deerhounds or the laughter of a girl. 'Nothing wrong with any of them,' says Fionn. 'But there's better music.' So they ask him what it is and he gives them his answer. 'The best music in the world,' he says, 'is the music of what happens.'

There are six ash trees here in Neillí's garden. Three were set by Paddy. Two more were set by Wilf. Five years ago the sixth one appeared from nowhere, seeded by the wind. There are three apple trees, set by Louis Mulcahy, and two pear trees, set by Wilf. Mike George gave us two alders and Wilf bought two others. He set them behind the byre and by the gate. There are five pollarded willow trees, grown from cuttings from the ditches. And six sycamore seedlings that came to us from Jack.

Mike George gave us the May trees you can see from the bedroom window. There's another one, from Enniscorthy, near the dogwood by the reeds. Jeant Ó Cinnéide swapped us the fir tree for several hydrangeas; he drove them back to Smerwick in the bucket of his JCB, and set them there in his garden below Binn Diarmada. Out by the road here are three hazel trees in a circle. They were set by Wilf and my brother and they came to us from Mike George. I count those trees now and I know how they came here. They weren't part of a plan. They're part of the music of what happens.

The hydrangeas were the riotous pink ones we found when we first came here. Wilf dug most of them out with a pickaxe and we gave them to the neighbours. I don't think we'll ever have the immaculate garden that people here remember from Con's time. But I hope he'd be pleased to know his hydrangeas flower now in Smerwick, up in Márthain, back in Glaise Beag and over in Clogher; and in a high garden in Baile na hAbha, looking over Dún Chaoin, and out to the islands. They still bloom in the hedges round Tí Neillí Mhuiris as well. I did my best to displace the pink and ensure we kept the blue ones. But I failed. And now, in winter, their dried heads, on grey-white stalks, fade to dusty crimson and grey-purple, and light dark corners of the house.

Yesterday Wilf and I walked up Mount Eagle. It was a shining day after a week of rain. From the top of the Clasach there's a steep stony path, narrow, and deep in the centre, cleft into the mountain like the bed of a stream. It curves from north to south around the side of the mountain. On either side of the path, clumps of purple heather starred with tiny white wildflowers grow in the boggy earth. On your left, where the mountain rises above you, the cleft's sliced a low cross section through earth and stone. Under the heather and star-flowers, exposed roots reach down to where black bog meets a layer of grey stone. A thin curtain of water streams down the low rock face, dripping from the wet earth above it and seeping deeper into the mountain through the loose stones under your feet. To your right, the mountain drops away through bogland and green fields towards Dún Chaoin and the blue ocean. The higher you climb, the wider your view of the horizon. Yesterday was a calm day. Miles below me, and miles out from the shore, a ferry was crossing to the island. A dot on the surface of the water with a forked wake streaming behind it. White foam against blue waves, like a swallow's tail against the sky.

Mount Eagle is the last peak on the peninsula's high mountain spine. After the steep climb from the Clasach, the path turns south-west round the mountain and becomes a wide bog-road. It's still rising but you hardly feel it. The climb becomes a walk. Further on it gets steeper again, as you climb to the summit. But by then your legs have got used to it, and it's easy to make it to the top. From the peak you can see for miles in all directions, with the ocean on three sides; it curves round the foot of the mountain from Smerwick Harbour on one side of the peninsula to Ventry Harbour on the other, and Dingle Harbour beyond. Out to the west, the islands wallow in the Atlantic like a whale surrounded by her young. Behind you, to the north-east, is Mount Brandon. The high clouds throw moving shadows on the earth and pale reflections on the ocean. The horizon's a silver thread in the distance. The valleys are bowls of golden light.

We sat together on Mount Eagle, eating goat's cheese

and sultana scones, apples and chocolate. We had water in a bottle that I'd filled from the kitchen tap; before it reached our kitchen it had been filtered by the mountain, through purple heather, white starflowers, black bog, and grey, fissured stone. I looked out to the west, with the wind on my face and a chunk of chocolate in my hand. Then the clouds shifted, the islands were furled in mist, and I remembered the bar of chocolate I ate on a high cliff on my first day here at Mrs Hurley's. That day, more than half a lifetime away, I had a glimpse of something I'm still looking for. Awareness in stillness.

When I first left Ireland for London I thought I just wanted to work in the theatre. But, looking back now, I know there was more. I wanted anonymity. In a foreign city where no one knows you, you can discover who you are. Hidden in a crowd, you can take risks and make mistakes and no one will notice. And without the baggage that comes with connections and relationships, you've got nothing to work with but yourself. When I went to London I wanted to learn my trade in a place where its values and standards were highest. It was like going to Spain if you're a bullfighter, or Silicon Valley if you're working in IT. But I think now that I was also looking for touchstones, to measure values and standards themselves. What I found led me full circle – back to Ireland and Corca Dhuibhne and a deeper exploration of the inheritance I'd left behind. I've moved from wanting anonymity to rediscovering identity; and from wanting things now to wanting to wait for them to happen in their own time. I'm learning to live in the present, and to know that I can't control what may come next. In finding a balance between our lives in these two places, I've found balance in my own health. And now each place informs the other, as each story I hear or tell sheds light on all the rest.

Yesterday when Wilf and I came down the mountain, we drove down the Clasach and round to the pottery café in Dún Chaoin. A group of kids on hired bikes had arrived before us. The bikes were piled by the door and, through the window, I could see the kids crowded round the counter ordering coffee and cake. Wilf sat outside on the wall and I went in to get tea. I came back with the teapot, a milk jug and two cups on a tray, a slice of rhubarb crumble, and two forks. As I closed the door with my elbow, a couple of German tourists got up from the table they'd been sitting at, and went in to look at the shop. Wilf moved from the wall to the table and I joined him with the tray. We sat where we've sat a hundred times before, drinking tea, sharing crumble and looking out at the island. And looking back on this book.

While I've been writing it, markets have slumped and banks and governments have crashed, but the unchanging wheel of the year has kept turning. There's a chill in the air today and the grass in the fields is beginning to melt back into the earth. Soon only foolhardy tourists will sit outside cafés as we once did, trying to hold on to summer by drinking tea in a gale. Yesterday, as we ate our rhubarb crumble, there was a flutter of wings overhead. I looked up to see swallows wheeling above us, preparing to migrate, their forked tails and white feathers echoing the foaming wake I'd seen from the mountain. As they swooped vertically from above I could see their wide beaks stretched to scoop up midges. Years ago I wrote a TV programme about birds, but there was an expert who did the science bits, and I didn't retain many facts. I do remember that at this time of year, swallows accumulate fat before migrating to South Africa. Some go through France, across the Pyrenees, along eastern Spain into Morocco and across the Sahara. Others follow the west coast of Africa, or make their way further east and down the Nile Valley. No one knows why they choose one route rather than another. Their lives may be richer and more complex than we know, but it seems they're programmed to function as a group and follow their instincts. People, on the other hand, make choices. We can each decide what we value and how we want to live.

This book started from the idea of the ancient Celts' world view, and the way they chose to preserve it. Celts didn't write books. In fact we know from Roman writers who had contact with them that the Celts disapproved of writing, because they believed it weakened their ability to remember. Instead of writing about their world view, they used memory as a tool for preserving and debating it. And they believed that remembering was a shared responsibility that bound communities together in a web of individual awareness.

But to the Greeks and Romans the Celts were 'uncivilised'. That's not surprising, because 'civilised', is a Latin word, meaning someone who lives in a city or town, from which society is ordered and administered. The ancient Celts were farmers who lived in tribes. They didn't build cities. But they did engineer roads, and they travelled immense distances. They seem to have started out east of the Rhine and expanded across huge areas, including much of Britain, Ireland, Belgium, France, the Netherlands, Portugal, Spain, Germany, Switzerland, Austria and Italy. They spread along the Danube towards the Black Sea, pressed on to Thrace and Macedonia and even made contact with the Scythians. At the height of ancient Celtic expansion an army of about twenty thousand crossed into Asia Minor, founded settlements in Galatia, in eastern Phrygia, and occupied the site of modern Ankara. And they did it without financial systems, writing, or administrative centres. Instead, their cultural identity was expressed across this vast territory by shared language, belief systems, customs and art. It was an extraordinary model for living, predating the Roman Empire by centuries. And in only a few generations it was forgotten.

Except that it wasn't. Fragmented and blurred by time, the essence of whatever the ancient Celts had to offer still survives in a few small pockets across Europe. Here in Corca Dhuibhne it's been remembered and handed on in a language that's been edging towards extinction for the last few hundred years. And since I've come to live here, I've learnt how much the language matters. The customs, and even the stories, can survive without it. So can carved stones and glass ring-beads, fluted twisted collars and hollow-hulled, gold boats. But they all came from a culture of telling and listening, remembering and passing things on. Here it was the Irish language that shaped all the layers of their meaning, and expressed them in words crafted by men and women whose lives were moulded by awareness. Of the poetry in physical skills; of the way one note in a tune sings to another; of the hugeness of the earth, the sky and the ocean, and the smallness of a wren's woven nest. It's awareness rooted in the belief that, since all things contain all other things, nothing that exists is unimportant. Because everything in the universe shares a living soul.

That world view's not unique to the Celts, but theirs is the version my neighbours here have inherited. It's my inheritance too, and in Tí Neillí Mhuiris I've begun to understand what it means to live with it. When I look back now to the night in Gorman's when we first thought of living here, I remember the saying I remembered from my childhood. 'When you understand where you've come from you'll be able to see where you're going.' For most of my life I've lived in a culture that values individuals more than communities and measures happiness in terms of physical appearance, success on a career ladder and acquisition of stuff. I've seen where the chase for that kind of happiness leads, and I don't want to go there. And here in Corca Dhuibhne, embedded in the Irish language, I've found possibilities for a different definition of happiness. Or at least for a different way of exploring what it might mean.

I thought of the first morning I woke up in Corca Dhuibhne when I heard Mrs Hurley's voice outside my door. '*Tá roinnt bricfeasta ullamh anois agam duit, a chailín.*' 'I have a share of breakfast ready now for you, girl.' I didn't know it then, but what I'd heard was a world view contained in an idiom: the food spread on the table wasn't my breakfast, it was my share of breakfast.

Nearly forty years later, here in Tí Neillí Mhuiris, I heard one of my neighbours talking about her grand-daughter. 'They have everything these days,' she said, '*ach n'fheadair a' bhfuil said sásta,*' 'but I don't know if they're happy.' There was a ripple of recognition round the room. Then someone asked for the secret of happiness. Heads nodded by the fire, and the women spoke almost in chorus, '*caithidís bheith sásta*'. If you've just learned that the word *sásta* means 'happy' that sounds odd; it's as if they were saying that to be happy you have to be happy. But in Irish, *sásta* contains a deeper meaning. People do use it when they're speaking about happiness. But it also means 'satisfied', or 'content'. People here know that too much or too little of anything means lack of balance. Balance brings contentment. And if no one takes more than their share in life, we can all be satisfied.

When we came to live here, Wilf and I weren't escaping from an English city to a rural Irish idyll. Life can be stressful wherever you live, and close communities breed their own tensions and frustrations. For us, living in two places wasn't about running from one and escaping to the other. It was about heightening our awareness and appreciation of both.

And that's what's happened. Each time life and work take me to London, there's a brief window – maybe just on the journey from the airport into town – when everything I see and hear becomes a touchstone. Air quality. No sense of earth, sea or sky. Old people expected to move faster than they're able. Dogs dragged through city crowds on leads. You walk the streets and you feel the groundswell of tension. People's nervousness round teenagers. People in restaurants scowling at mothers with babies. Commuters plugged into their iPods, using music to block out the world.

And then comes the second wave of awareness, and that's the music of what happens. A flutter of wings in a tree in the Old Kent Road. Soaring, glittering buildings by the Thames. Generations of skill crafted into Victorian tiles or the curve of an iron railing. An urban fox sauntering through the streets, living his own secret life in the midst of the commuters. And you see small, generous moments of human contact. People giving up seats on buses. Thanking each other. Laughing and chatting in shops. Strangers smiling at each other. Neighbours offering help. None of that might be obvious, but it's all there to be tapped into. It expresses the wholeness of the universe, and it offers endless entry-points to a shared sense of energy and strength.

Last night, up behind Tí Neillí Mhuiris, a new moon hung over the mountain. It was the turning point between moonset and sunrise and no dogs barked. In the grey garden the ash trees were black against the sky. Each leaf and each blade of grass was edged with dewdrops. I stood in the cold air, listening to silence. Air and water filtered silently through heather and starflowers, black bog and fissured stone. The mountain breathed in the darkness. And in my mind's eye, a hare in a high field turned his head to the moon.

Kill a calf, kill a cow.
There, my story's ended now.

Acknowledgements

I'm greatly indebted to Fenella Bates, my commissioning editor, for her personal enthusiasm and professional expertise; to all at Hodder & Stoughton and at Hachette Ireland; and – as ever – to my agent Gaia Banks at Sheil Land Associates.

My gratitude's also due to everyone whose stories and memories are retold here. I hope that my own memory has done justice to what's been shared with me.

Do you wish this wasn't the end?

Join us at www.hodder.co.uk, or follow us on
Twitter @hodderbooks to be a part of our community
of people who love the very best in books and reading.

Whether you want to discover more about a book
or an author, watch trailers and interviews, have the
chance to win early limited editions, or simply browse
our expert readers' selection of the very best books,
we think you'll find what you're looking for.

And if you don't,
that's the place to tell us what's missing.

We love what we do, and we'd love you to be part of it.

www.hodder.co.uk

@hodderbooks

HodderBooks

HodderBooks